TOP
TIPS
for Life

By Kate Reardon

Top Tips for Girls
Top Tips for Life

TOP
TIPS
for Life

KATE
REARDON

__headline__

First published in 2010
by HEADLINE PUBLISHING GROUP

This edition published in 2010
by HEADLINE PUBLISHING GROUP

1

Cataloguing in Publication Data is available from the British Library

ISBN 978 0 7553 6021 5

Typeset in Garamond3 by Avon DataSet Ltd, Warwickshire
Printed and bound in Great Britain by Clays Ltd, St Ives plc

HEADLINE PUBLISHING GROUP
An Hachette UK Company
338 Euston Road, London NW1 3BH

www.headline.co.uk
www.hachette.co.uk
www.TopTips.com

For my friends.
Thank you for letting me pick you.

Kate Reardon has spent twenty years at the cutting edge of women's publishing. She started as a fashion student at American *Vogue* and at twenty-one was made Fashion Editor of *Tatler*. She has contributed to most of the UK's national newspapers and written three columns in *The Times* – who named her one of Britain's best writers. She is currently a Contributing Editor at *Vanity Fair*.

Kate founded TopTips.com in 2007. She is a major fundraiser for Cancer Research UK. Kate divides her time between London and Wiltshire, and is saving up for a horse.

CONTENTS

TOP TIPS FOR LIFE

REAL ADVICE FROM REAL WOMEN FOR REAL LIFE

Introduction

There are two types of women: those who are a bit vague and non-committal when you ask what delicious perfume they're wearing; and those who, when they discover an exciting new method of hair removal, demand that you feel their newly-smooth lower leg and examine it minutely for any vestiges of hair as they dial the therapist to make an appointment for you.

The website TopTips.com is very much for and written by the latter sort of woman. It is a community of women who don't feel that life is a giant competition, nor that another woman's success (whether it be at work or at hair removal) diminishes them in any way. It attracts women who actually like other women, and who enjoy giving each other advice.

Welcome to *Top Tips for Life*, the second book of practical, funny and brilliant tips gleaned from TopTips.com. Since the first book was published, tens of thousands of tips have been submitted to the site, so it would be daft not to put the best into a second volume. There are even more hard-won words of wisdom on an extraordinary range of subjects, from how to calm a screaming baby, to how to react when you find naughty texts on your partner's mobile, or how to make perfect meat balls, or how to find a suitable male in later life. And there are two new and exciting categories that apply to everyone: friendship and happiness.

The friendship chapter (covering everything from how to be a good friend to how to support a pal going through chemotherapy) was prompted by the following exchange: someone posted the problem, 'How to turn little friendships into true ones when you need a shoulder to cry on?' I was gob-smacked and delighted when a tipster called Pienkfly replied, 'Let me give you the perfect answer. We at TopTips are your TRUE best friends. We are here 24/7. So, if you need to cry, we are just a click away. I subscribed to this website on 18 March 2008, and you know what, I submitted my problems, and got so many true, straight answers and solutions. Although we don't know each other, we give you honest help. Some friends lie to one another just to make them feel better, we don't.'

One of the benefits of TopTips.com is that it's as anonymous as you want it to be – women discuss anxieties which they wouldn't dare voice even to their best friend. Written and read by women from all over the world, it allows them to post problems (from the prosaic to the profound) and those with a view post their suggested solutions. Encouraging users to leave something handy behind when they go, TopTips. com is the agony aunt who allows you to be the aunt and the agonee.

This book is the result of a collaboration between all the thousands of fabulously bossy women who have submitted advice on TopTips.com. Editing it was not easy: starting with a spreadsheet of 26,000 often brilliant tips which had been submitted since the last book was compiled, I whittled it down to about 800. I would be happy if I never had to click that little green Excel icon ever again.

A word of warning: I haven't tested them all, so if you follow any of the advice, think it through a bit first. If a tip doesn't work, or you end up turning your toenails green, please let me and the rest of the world know by going to TopTips. com – so we can get it right for the next book.

WITH THANKS TO

Renee Joyce at our online developers Tangent. She is the buffer between me and the tech team. Her patience and good nature in the face of sometimes maddening technical issues are awe-inspiring. (For those of you who don't work in the online world:

websites are never finished and bugs crop up for no apparent reason – it's like your fridge spontaneously unplugs itself to go and sit in your bathroom every time your back is turned.)

Kate Lee and Karolina Sutton at ICM and Curtis Brown respectively. They are wonderful women, without whom these books would have been a pipe dream.

Carly Cook at Headline; she is a new and brilliant ally.

The fabulous Abi Chisman and the sensational David Lindsay.

Intrusive Derek.

All the tipsters who visit TopTips.com and daily share their wisdom and advice. LindaCee, Jillaroo95 and DezG deserve special mentions – they are consistently brilliant, insightful and funny.

All the celebrities who have so generously shared their own Top Tips, especially on the topic of happiness.

My mother, who has always had a slightly irritating obsession with the correct use of language (inherited from her own mother, and which, I suspect, she is transferring to me by osmosis). Bored with fruitlessly fighting it, I harnessed that obsession and asked for her help in editing this book. Here is an exchange of our emails when she had finished correcting the spelling and grammar.

> **From:** <u>Polly Wood</u>
> **To:** <u>Kate Reardon</u>
> **Sent:** Thursday, July 23, 2009 7:35 PM
> **Subject:** finished
> DONE.
> OK, so what do I get?

> **From:** <u>Kate Reardon</u>
> **To:** <u>Polly Wood</u>
> **Sent:** Friday, July 24, 2009 10:34 AM
> **Subject:** Re: finished

My eternal love and gratitude, and the satisfaction of a job well done, as well as knowing that you are continuing to fulfil your motherly obligations to the full.

: -)

THANK YOU

From: <u>Polly Wood</u>
To: <u>Kate Reardon</u>
Sent: Friday, July 24, 2009 10:40 AM
Subject: Re: Re: finished

Ah yes. Slipped my mind.

BEAUTY

or It's not all in the eye of the beholder

How to not look tired

Try massaging your ears with your thumb and forefinger.
Start at the top and massage firmly all over your ears and
earlobes. Do it whenever you need to perk up! Sounds
silly, but it works.

DUSTY

How to look more friendly

I always smile if I catch someone's eye. It takes a hard-
faced beggar not to acknowledge a smile freely given.
And remember not to frown as you walk down the street.

MAMAMBYTH

How to look younger

The easiest, cheapest, fastest way to look younger is to
stand up straight. You can take ten years off your look
by pulling your shoulders down and your stomach in.
Make this a habit when you walk down the street, and no
matter how old you are, it will take years off.

KATHCONN

How to get that perfect eyebrow shape

Have them tattooed by an expert, either permanently or semi-permanently. With the former, don't go for too dark a colour as they must match your skin as time goes by. The process hurts like hell but there are products you can get to numb the skin beforehand and it's really worth it.

CALI

How to apply false eyelashes

Don't put the glue directly on to the false eyelashes. Instead put a small blob on the back of your hand and then lightly slide or pull your false eyelashes through it. This stops you using too much glue.

PINKFLUFFYDEE

How to use eyelash curlers

Instead of holding eyelashes down with your curlers just once, do it three times, starting from the base, then the middle, and then the tips, holding for about fifteen seconds.

FRANKIEFACE

How to apply eyeliner without smudging

Apply a thin line of your face powder around your eye with a stiff-angled eyeliner brush and apply your eyeliner over the top. Don't use eye cream before applying eyeliner – if you need something try a gel that is less oily and less likely to cause smudges.

SARAHFAIRY

I use an eyebrow pencil instead; it doesn't smudge as easily and stays put for longer.

MARRANT

How to sharpen eyeliner pencils without them breaking

To stop your eyeliner pencils breaking or snapping when you sharpen them, put them in the freezer for a minute or two before sharpening. Works a treat.

JESS5377

How to find an eye shadow base that actually keeps its promise

I usually use my foundation as a base. You can dab as much as you want with your finger all over your eyelid or just where you need it. It's affordable and it works.

HOOPZ

How to prevent oily eyelids which ruin eye shadow

A very effective, thrifty option is to powder your eyelids with face powder.

SARAHFAIRY

How to make your eyes look bigger

Use a light colour eye shadow in the inner corner of your eye, and get darker as you go further out. Also use eyelash curlers; they really open up your eyes.

XXHAZELXX

Use white eye pencil on the inner, lower lids. It will highlight the eye colour too.

MARRANT

How to get the most from expensive face creams

Before applying your face cream, make sure your face is
completely dry. If there's any water on the surface, it will
dilute the product you are applying.

SOPHIEO8

How to save on face packs and have glossy hair

My mother always used up any cracked eggs by using the
whites as a face pack and applying the yolks on her hair
to make it look glossy. Nothing wasted.

HOUSEGOOSE

How to make a face mask for oily skin

Milk of Magnesia is excellent for oily and acne-prone
skin – you will see a difference almost immediately.
Apply every night using cotton wool; let it dry for ten
minutes, and then wash off as normal.

FRIQBAL

How to make natural bath oil

Get a cheap bottle of almond oil from the chemist and
add a few drops of your favourite essential oils – my
personal favourites are rose, lavender and geranium.
Shake it up and pour in your bath! Alternatively, pop
a few sprigs of rosemary or lavender in your bottle of
almond oil, close tightly, and let it infuse for a week or
so – you will end up with a lovely bath oil. You could
decant it into a pretty bottle and display it in your
bathroom or use as a gift. Make sure you use only woody,
tough herbs for this, like rosemary and lavender. Things
like rose petals or fruit peel will discolour and go bad,
and will look ugly if left by the bath.

SARAHFAIRY

How to reduce the appearance of stretched ear piercings

Wearing heavy, dangling earrings over a long time can cause your earlobe piercings to stretch. This looks horrible but you can 'fix' it invisibly. Just cut a small piece of surgical tape or a strip of plaster big enough to cover the hole, place it on the back of the earlobe, then carefully put the earring stem through the plaster support. It's as if you have a brand new piercing. Change it daily.

LESLEY998

How to have great lashes on a budget

With mascara, I've found it's how you prepare the lashes that adds drama, as some of the most expensive mascaras don't live up to their claims. Use eyelash curlers to give your lashes great curl, then build up the coats of mascara, separating each with a good lash comb.

MARRANT

How to set foundation

Wait a good five minutes between putting on your moisturiser and applying your foundation. Makes a big difference and seems to give you a better canvas to build on.

PINKBUNNYGIRL

How to stop lipstick bleeding

When putting on your make-up, apply foundation to your lips as well. This will prevent lipstick from bleeding.

MICHELE0810

How to prevent wrinkles around your eyes

Smear a good layer of Vaseline around your eyes at night. It totally works.

JEMZIE

How to get gorgeous cuticles

Rub a drop of olive oil into each cuticle.

CHOCOLATENOOR

How to grow long, strong nails

Try taking glucosamine supplements daily. They are relatively inexpensive and, if you take them every day, within a month your nails will be noticeably stronger (and your skin and hair will be better too!).

MYSPANDEX

How to guard against smudging your pedicured toenails

It's simple, but easily forgotten: for pedicures, wear flip-flops to the salon.

LINDACEE

How to give yourself a great manicure

Before you paint your nails, even if you don't need to remove old polish, go over your nails with a cotton wool pad soaked in nail polish remover. This removes any traces of dirt, oil, soap, hand cream, etc., which otherwise would stop the polish from adhering properly to your nails.

NJDAVIE2

How to make acrylic overlays last longer

Use nail oil. As soon as you get back from the salon, massage lots in and around your nails and cuticles – this seems to stop any cracking or lifting. Then repeat every night if you can. And whenever you are using bleach or limescale remover, etc., wear rubber gloves, as that stuff will permeate your nails in no time and make the overlays lift.

BLONDEARIESCHICK

How to stop biting your nails

Try giving up a nail at a time.

LEXIELOU

I've bitten my nails my whole life and this is the only thing that has worked: buy a big pack of cheap false nails (I got one from my local beauty store with ten sets in the pack) and wear them. Cut them short and paint them so they look natural and you can still use your hands. Change the nails every three days, and by the time you've used up all the sets of nails, your own nails will have grown.

CARAMELFRAPP

Every morning after eating breakfast scrape your nails along a bar of soap and then go about your day. Every time you go to bite your nails, you'll know about it.

NATUREFIRST

How to clear up spots

I used to suffer with acne and tried every kind of lotion and potion until it dawned on me that a natural remedy would be best. After a lot of research, I found out that a honey face mask works wonders! Simple as that – smear honey over your whole face, leave for twenty minutes and wash off with water. Within a few weeks, you really notice the difference.

BROWNGIRL

Tea tree oil contains terpinen-4, a compound that fights harmful bacteria and fungi. This ingredient makes tea tree oil an effective treatment against acne.

CALLISTA

How to get whiter teeth as naturally as possible

Dip your brush into bicarbonate of soda and brush your teeth. This is an abrasive and removes coffee and red wine stains.

REDLADY

How to get food out of your teeth when you are nowhere near a toothbrush

On those awful occasions when I've had food caught in my teeth and haven't been near floss, I've used . . . a staple. Really. Punch the stapler once to release a staple and use that.

JILLAROO95

BODY

or Either do something about it or shut up

How to be confident with your body, especially when naked in front of someone special

Remember the rule of thumb: look at your thumb now, and what do you see? Just a thumb, right? OK, so it might be a little short, or the nail might not be filed to perfection, but really, it's just a thumb. Now when you are naked in front of your boyfriend, just remember your thumb, and remember that he's not seeing your short bits or big bits or little bits or whatever, he's just praising the Lord that there is a naked woman, no matter what she looks like, standing in front of him.

PRINCESS MISCHA

How to beat cellulite

This won't stop the problem but if you do it for long enough it will help: before leaving your shower, spray your cellulite with really cold water for as long as you can bear.

HELLOIMCHARLI

With a dry body brush, brush your body with upward strokes towards your heart, then exfoliate in the shower and moisturise when you get out.

VBULLIMORE

I have been massaging vitamin E oil into my damn
thighs morning and night for the last three days, and it's
made a pronounced difference to my cellulite already. I
also take it as a supplement.

GRETCHEN

Scoot along your carpet on your bum fifty times – it
makes the blood circulate and is really effective.

RILEYKO5

How to prevent stretch marks

My mum (God rest her soul) told me that the best way
to prevent stretch marks is to massage in extra virgin
olive oil. She had five children, no stretch marks and
great skin at eighty-six.

MILOU

How to get soft feet

After you have done your pedicure and slathered your
feet in moisturiser, wrap your feet in cling film and put
on a pair of old socks. If you can bear it, sleep in them.
If not, wear for a couple of hours – your feet will be
amazingly soft.

JoMALONE

How to get rid of corns or calluses

Wrap your toes in plasters at all times when wearing
shoes or slippers. Never cut corns or calluses or rub them
with pumice stones or files. Corns and calluses are ways
for your feet or hands to protect themselves from friction,
so if you apply friction by rubbing them, they will never
go away. The skin will normalise when pressure is no
longer applied to it. Be patient, it could take up to a
year, depending on the size of the corn.

DEANNADOLLSON

How to apply fake tan to your back when you've got nobody to help

Apply as much of the tan as you can on your lower back, the back of your shoulders, etc. Then use the back of your hand (not your palm) to rub it in the middle/top area of your back. It works for me – although I don't think that clicking noise in my shoulder is normal, eek!

TASHNU53

How to remove fake tan without scrubbing

Nail varnish remover usually does the trick!

CHESSY2

Use hair removal cream – it removes fake tan from legs and also removes hairs, so a two-in-one bonus!

ANNIEBELL

How to calm itchy hair re-growth after epilation

It helps to exfoliate the day before hair removal. If you still get itchy skin, a cotton wool pad soaked in witch hazel cools and calms and works a treat, and it's very cheap. (It also works well on spots.)

PICKLEDPARSNIP

How to beat shaving rash

If you shave your legs when you are slightly cold, you will probably have goose bumps and so will damage the skin, making it itchy and broken afterwards. So the next time you shave, make sure you are warm enough.

BOO

How to get a super-smooth shave on your legs

To achieve super-smooth legs, run a bath to soften the hairs, exfoliate, then use a little olive oil (instead of shaving gel). This works wonders. The razor will glide smoothly, leaving legs free of cuts, and they'll feel well moisturised afterwards.

ALIXGB

After shaving, run your hands up your legs to feel for any remaining hair or rough bits.

EVANESCENCE100

How to make dry hands soft

I use almond oil to soften my hands. It also does wonders for your nails by preventing them from splitting and cracking. Just apply a small drop and rub in well at night and after any contact with water containing detergent. It's very inexpensive and available from loads of chemists.

KGIRL

How to make your hands smooth and prevent them bleeding in cold weather

I've had this for years and I know it is EXTREMELY painful! Try using a castor oil/zinc cream (or any other cream for babies' bums) just before bedtime. Cover up with the plastic gloves from a home hair colouring kit. The plastic makes your hands sweat a lot, but they absorb the cream better. Try to do this as a special weekly treatment all year long and not just when your hands are bleeding.

JILLY14

How to stop your knees and elbows ageing before the rest of you

Exfoliate knees and elbows with a mixture of olive oil and salt, then moisturise.

REDLADY

How to find a washing powder that is good for sensitive skin

Try a soap powder for baby clothing as this is always good for sensitive skin.

SASSY

How to cure or prevent a rash under a heavy bust

Get yourself fitted for a new bra – your breasts should NOT be hanging down against the skin below (and I say this as a GG-cupper who had exactly this problem when wearing the wrong size in the past).

DISTRACTEDHOUSEWIFE

Wash under breast and dry thoroughly. Then, using a powder puff, apply Vagisil powder all over the area that gets affected. It will keep the skin dry all day, unlike ordinary talc, and therefore the warm, damp conditions that allow growth of the microscopic fungus that causes the rash don't occur. If, despite this, you still get an occasional rash, use 1% clotrimazole cream (e.g. Canesten cream) or, if the rash is persistent, use hydrocortisone cream (e.g. Daktacort cream).

SALLYSPROGGS

How to stop thighs rubbing and chafing when wearing a skirt in hot weather

Talcum powder should do the trick.

MACKIEOX

How to prevent people staring at your chest

You could try saying, 'Oh! Have I spilt something on my top?'

ATOPGIRL

How to enjoy your breasts and dress sexily without making men feel uncomfortable

The secret is to make sure you're wearing a really good bra that 'contains' your breasts. You can then wear low-cut tops and dresses without that horrible wobbly spillage. Basically, it's about choosing the right time and place to flash the flesh. A night out on the town? Yes. A Wednesday morning in the office? No.

TIZZYSMUM

HAIR

or If they can put a man on the moon,
why can't they fix the frizzies?

How to get gum out of your hair

A very simple way to get gum out of hair is to drench
it in olive oil. I promise, it works every time. Work it
into the hair and gum, and then you can just slide the
gum out.

BRIANNE

How to tame flyaway and static hair

All you need to do is spread a little of your lip-gloss or
lip balm over your hands and gently wipe over the frizz.

KIMBERLEY

Just spray a little hairspray on your brush before using.

PATSHARP

How to use unwanted conditioner

I have thick hair and use conditioner as you would a
serum. It really controls my hair and keeps frizz at bay.

REDLADY

How to give more volume to your hair

Backcomb! I swear by it, but don't go over the top. Just lift your hair up and backcomb the bits underneath to give more volume and the impression of thicker hair. Spray on some hairspray when finished and *voilà*, thick hair.

xXxLeannexXx

How to add volume to dull, flat hair

To wake up tired, flat hair, spray hairspray on your fingertips and massage through your roots – it works a treat!

AuntyV

How to find a good stylist for long hair

If you're brave enough, stop somebody in the street whose hair length/colour is similar to yours and whose style you like, and ask her which stylist she goes to. Anyone would be pleased and flattered to be approached in this way and a personal recommendation is worth way more than an advert.

DISTRACTEDHOUSEWIFE

How to get hair dye off your skin

Hairspray or nail varnish remover gets hair dye off, but be very careful to protect your eyes.

RENCHA

How to get strong hair

I am Pakistani and my mum always massaged either
coconut or almond oil into my scalp and told me to keep
it on all day or overnight. The trick to this is to wear
a shower cap and use a towel on your pillow at night.
When you're done, shampoo twice and condition very
lightly.

CHOCOLATENOOR

How to make hair grow faster

I massage my head for three minutes every time
I shampoo and condition my locks. I never cut it
(sometimes the very ends get a teeny trim). Cutting hair
every few weeks may stop split ends but it certainly does
not make it grow any faster. I also use home-made olive
oil and beer hair masks. Mix it up, slather it on, bung
a hot, damp towel around it, watch half an hour of TV,
rinse out (thoroughly) and you too can have hair down to
your hips like mine.

LADYDIGGER

How to get rid of the greasy residue left after
using lice lotion

A vinegar rinse should take care of this. Lemon juice is
also good and smells better but vinegar rinses out more
easily. Buy a big bottle of malt vinegar and apply it
carefully after shampooing, paying particular attention
to the roots and scalp. Then rinse. A lot.

ROSEBUDSMUMMY

How to keep swimmers' hair conditioned and shiny

If you're a regular swimmer and find it wreaks havoc on the condition of your hair: always wear a swimming cap, but before donning it, saturate your hair in conditioner. After a half-hour swim you can hit the shower and wash your hair in your usual way. Your hair will have benefited from an intensive 'treatment' helped by the heat generated from your exercise – works for me!

ANTOINETTE

How to make clip-in hair extensions stay in

Backcomb your hair a little just in the place where the clips will sit. This will give them something to hold on to.

IMI

How to remove hair product residue

Once a week, add a tablespoon of baking soda to your shampoo and conditioner. Your hair feels so much cleaner!

CHOCOLATENOOR

How to spot the difference between shampoo and conditioner in the shower if you are short-sighted

Write a big 'C' and a big 'S' on the appropriate bottles using coloured nail varnish or marker pen.

PaulineGG

How to stop getting greasy hair (if leaving it unwashed for several days doesn't work)

Try washing it without scrubbing or rubbing your hair at all. Just use diluted shampoo, pour it over your head and stroke it in gently. This will stop your scalp from being over-stimulated and should ease the problem over time.

BIANCA

How to prevent hair going wavy in damp weather

My science teacher told me that if you use wax products VERY sparingly on your hair it acts as a barrier to the water in humidity.

KIRSTIE123

STYLE

or Maybe I'd better wear jeans after all

How to store small earrings

Buy a pill sorter box and keep small earrings in it – the sections are just the right size.

REDLADY

How to look pulled together at all times

Take a few minutes on a Sunday evening with your diary and decide what you need for the week: X amount of work outfits, Y amount of social outfits. Make up the combinations you like on separate hangers, together with underwear and accessories. The first time you do this it may take a little longer, but you will get it down to ten minutes max. This helps you to use all of your wardrobe, in different and sometimes unthought-of combinations. Notice what you don't wear and get creative with what you have. Saves money too.

ASHLING

How to avoid fashion emergencies

If you have a few handbags you use all the time fill a pocket in each with emergency supplies – safety pins, plasters, painkiller, lip balm, hair bands, etc.

LauraBailey

How to get new clothes out of old clothes

Find a tailor or seamstress you feel you can trust –
one who measures carefully and pins gently! Take in
clothes you love but which need some sprucing up. The
seamstress will be able to recommend what can be done
to give the garment new life – perhaps nipping in the
waist, subtly changing the collar, shortening the sleeves,
or whatever. I did this some years ago with about twenty
garments. For under a hundred pounds, I had what felt
like twenty new items of clothing. It's definitely worth
the price to extend the life of your existing clothes
without getting completely bored with them.

CEEVEE

How to get rid of static on clothes

Rub a dryer sheet over the clothes, even a used one will
work.

STELLADORE

How to know if you need to wear a bra

When you run, do they move up and down? Time for a
bra.

JILLAROO95

How to make yourself more noticeable

It's simple – if you want to get noticed, wear red! I
pulled this trick off the other day: I went to a meeting
where I wanted to be interviewed by someone from the
press about an issue that is very important to me, so I
wore my red coat. Who was the first person the press
came to? That's right, the woman in the red coat!

BEKKI007

How to rip/distress a pair of old jeans

Use sandpaper. You can use it to distress the denim gradually until you get the effect you want.

UBER

When distressing jeans, put them in the wash after customising, as it will help to create that soft, frayed edge.

JONES22

How to secure buttons

Cover the top of your buttons with a layer of clear nail varnish. The loose bits of cotton will stay secure and you won't be tempted to pick them! This is not suitable for buttons that are sewn on underneath or where you can't see any stitching.

ELIZABETHCOTEMAN

How to wear a backless halter-neck dress without looking flat-chested because you can't wear a padded bra

Get cups to sew into the dress! You can probably get them at a fabric store. That's what my tailor did for my wedding dress and it was really comfortable.

KENOSKO

How to really clear out your closet

Make an appointment for a charity to pick up unneeded clothes twice a year when you switch over your summer and winter clothes. It's a great way to de-clutter, get a fresh start and feel good – all in one!

CKHOKIEO2

How to decide which shoes to keep when downsizing your shoe collection

For the next month each time you wear a pair of shoes put them away the wrong way around. At the end of the month you will see exactly which shoes you really wear. The rest you will need to make a judgment call on.

MAUDE

How to remember great outfits

Whenever you wear an outfit you particularly like or get complimented on, take a picture of it and stick the picture on the inside of your closet door.

CHOCOLATENOOR

How to be organised if you use several handbags

Buy yourself some see-through bags with zips or small make-up bags. Put all your personal maintenance stuff into one and all your 'travelling' things like pens and pencils into the other. Not only will this make your handbag a whole lot tidier, but you can also move the bags quickly from one handbag to another and get more use out of your handbag collection.

LIZZIECRAIG

How to store handbags so you can see and access them easily in a small space

I've put a small rail with 'S' hooks (think kitchen storage at Ikea!) on the back of my bedroom door. This is perfect for small evening-type bags. You can get larger rails for larger bags that could be installed along a wall.

TOOMANYSHOES

How to straighten the brim of a straw hat

Hold it over the hot steam from a kettle (but be careful) and mould it back into shape.

ALII61

If the brim is supposed to be flat (like a boater-type should be), place it on a flat surface, weigh the brim down with heavy books, and leave somewhere warm for a few days. That should straighten it out.

SEAGULL-PIE

How to be organised for quick repairs

In a sewing kit keep three or four needles threaded in different colours to match your clothes. Keep the kit in your closet. That way when you take off your clothes in the evening and notice a button loose or hem unravelling, you can fix it quickly. You're more likely to do on-the-spot repairs if you have the needle and thread ready to hand.

ASHLING

How to fix a hem in an emergency

Adhesive dressing tape from the first aid kit works really well – it's flexible, so you won't get a weird rigid line.

DISTRACTEDHOUSEWIFE

How to fix a loose thread on a sweater

For pulling tugged threads through to the back of knitwear, a fine crochet hook is better than a needle. Just slide it through the jumper, 'hook' the errant thread and pull it back, with no need for fiddly needle threading. I keep a tiny crochet hook in my handbag for just this type of emergency – it's surprising how useful they are.

DISTRACTEDHOUSEWIFE

How to get rid of bobbles from wool and cashmere

Shave them off with a dry disposable razor.

ASHLEAP

How to get cocktail spills out of a rabbit-fur coat which has gone all sticky

It sounds like you have a fun life . . . Unless you want to take it to a specialist cleaner, I would do what a rabbit would do and wash it off gently using plain water. Although maybe you might want to use a dampened sponge instead of your tongue.

TOOKE

How to stop a ladder in your tights

If it's already slightly laddered use Sellotape on the inside of the tights to stop it getting bigger.

XSAMMYX

Wet a bar of soap very slightly and then rub around the ladder. When the soap dries, it will act like starch and stiffen, thus stopping the ladder/hole spreading. I have used this on many occasions and it never fails.

LADYDIGGER

How to remove odours from vintage clothes when dry cleaning doesn't work

Try rubbing dry bicarbonate of soda into the affected areas. Leave for about two hours, then brush off thoroughly. Repeat the process if the smell lingers. It worked on my coat.

LADYDIGGER

How to keep socks, tights etc. tidy

I put each pair of tights in its own little clear bag, such
as a food bag, and label it with a description such as
black opaque, diamond, fishnet, etc. This helps identify
them quickly as they all look the same when they are in a
mess in my drawer.

PRINCESS87

How to clean light-coloured suede or nubuck shoes

Take the soft bit from the centre of a piece of bread,
squash it, then lightly rub it over any stains to lift them.

MIMI18

How to get water stains off leather boots

First, clean the area with saddle soap, rinse using a damp,
soft cloth, and dry. Then lightly apply mink oil (you can
find suppliers easily through the internet) and rub into
all areas affected. This softens the leather and helps seal
against more staining, making the next cleaning easier.
If you want, get a can of sealer/protectant and spray all
outer areas of the boots. (The mink oil and/or the sealer
spray may darken the colour a little.)

333ROBIN

How to make the bottom of shoes unslippy

Put on the bottom of each shoe one of those decals –
decorative stickers (usually flowers or shells) that stop
you slipping in the bath.

CSTAR_I

How to stop a shoe from squeaking

Try putting talcum powder in the shoes. It makes your feet smell nice too.

BLONDIE5

How to stop your feet from slipping out of your shoes

If your shoes slip off your foot at the back as you walk/dance, spray the area with firm-hold hairspray just before you put them on.

DISTRACTEDHOUSEWIFE

How to stretch shoes

If your shoes are made of a natural fabric, pack them tightly with wet newspaper. As the newspaper dries, the paper expands and stretches the shoe slightly. If your shoes are man-made, the fabric may split if you attempt to stretch them too much.

DINGDONGTHEWITCH

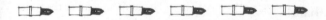

COOKING

or This has never happened to me before, I promise

How to avoid lumps in white sauce

Sieve the flour as you add it – this helps to prevent the lumps forming in the first place. If you do get lumps, use a whisk on the sauce before adding more liquid, and it should come out smooth.

MEREDITH TANGLE

How to get crackling crisp when roasting pork

Score the fat and then rub with oil and salt. Really crispy crackling!

REDLADY

How to get an onion or garlic smell off your hands

A catering trade secret: wash your hands afterwards in white wine or vinegar (if you don't mind the smell!).

ABI1973

How to get rid of 'chilli burns' on your hands after chopping chillies

The antidote for chilli is sugar. Dilute some in warm water and soak your hands in it. Rub Vaseline in afterwards.

ALI161

How to get a fish smell off your hands

Rub your hands under the tap with a stainless steel spoon or any stainless steel item. This works for garlic smells as well.

JADSIA

How to get a gorgeous finish on an iced cake

Once you've iced the cake, no matter what type of icing used, aim a blow dryer at it, turning the cake as you go. The heat will melt the icing ever so slightly, giving it a beautifully uniform and smooth finish.

CeeVee

How to avoid spattering when frying

Before frying, dry your food with a piece of paper towel – it's excess water that causes the spattering. Patted dry food always browns nicely too. Also, try not to use too much cooking oil.

CHERYLSAIGEON

How to cook a cooked breakfast without making a mess

Put the bacon, sausages, tomatoes and mushrooms in a roasting tin and drizzle with oil. Cook in the oven for fifteen minutes while you shower and dress. Turn the sausages and bacon, crack the eggs into spaces in the roasting tin, and put back in the oven for ten to fifteen minutes. Make the toast and put your lippy on.

DISTRACTEDHOUSEWIFE

How to cook aubergines so they are melt-in-the-mouth

It's not the cooking method, it's the preparation. They need to be 'sweated' to make them less tough and bitter. Put some paper towels on a plate. Slice the aubergines about a third-of-an-inch thick, then salt each slice on both sides, and place them on the paper towels. Layer them with the paper towels between each layer, and then put another plate on top of the whole thing and something on top to weigh it all down, and stick it in the refrigerator. Do this in the morning and by dinnertime, you'll have tender aubergines that you can cook any way you like.

JILLAROO95

How to cook basmati rice that isn't sticky and overcooked

Our Chinese amah in Singapore taught me this fifty years ago. It is completely foolproof. Put the rice into lots of boiling water, and cook for fourteen minutes (the rice should still be covered in water). Pour the rice through a sieve, and immediately run cold water over it, until the rice is cold. Cover and leave until serving time. Then pour a kettleful of boiling water through it, and serve. Result: large, fluffy, dry grains with a minimum of starch.

CANOPUS

How to cook the perfect soft-boiled egg

I put the egg (room temperature) into a pan of cold water, bring it to the boil and, once the water is bubbling, cook for two minutes. This is perfect for a soft-boiled medium-size egg. Add thirty seconds for a large egg. Also, slice off the top straightaway after removing it from the water, otherwise it will keep cooking. If it's slightly too runny, pop the sliced-off top back on and leave for a minute or so; it will have cooked a little more and should be just right.

MEREDITH TANGLE

How to cool down hot oatmeal in a delicious and healthy way

In the summer, when fresh fruit is plentiful, lightly rinse, dry and coarsely chop up lots of fruit, then freeze it. In the cooler months, if you're making hot cereal, pop a few frozen berries into the cereal. It will cool the oatmeal down enough to eat and also add flavour, fibre and colour to your breakfast.

CEEVEE

How to remove fat from soup or gravy quickly and easily

Heat the soup until very hot. Pour it into a heatproof bowl or measuring cup, and then cover the soup's surface with ice cubes. Wait three to five minutes, and then give it a gentle stir. The fat will solidify into little globules and cling to the ice cubes. Remove and discard the ice cubes, and you've removed the vast majority of the fat.

CEEVEE

Leave overnight in the fridge. The fat will rise to the top and you can skim it off. This is useful with stews and casseroles, too (which often taste better the next day anyway).

PATSHARP

How to stop the skin forming on your sauce or gravy

My mother always puts cling film over the surface of sauces and takes it off just before serving – it really works!

LUCYD

How to cut a large quantity of uncooked meat easily

Stick the meat in the freezer for twenty minutes before cutting it. This makes it much easier to cut, and much easier to trim away the fat.

CEEVEE

How to eat healthily on a tight budget

Check your butcher or supermarket for meat offers and freeze any extra portions. Pulses and beans are another inexpensive protein option. Get a slow cooker if you can; it's cheap to run, can be ignored while cooking, will cook tougher ends of meat and make them tender. It's the best kitchen investment you can make for efficiency and economy.

ASHLING

How to find or cook tasty food that is low in salt or sodium

There are a number of herb and spice mixes that are marketed as salt replacements. Also, cook with garlic – it's good for the heart and adds wonderful flavour to food.

JILLAROO95

How to get all the bits of shell out of seafood

If you have to sort through crab or lobster meat to pick out the random bits of shell, spread the meat out on a baking sheet, and stick it in an oven at 180°C/350°F/Gas Mark 4 for just three to four minutes. All the shell bits will turn opaque and will be easy to see and pick out! (This doesn't actually cook the meat.)

CEEVEE

How to grate cheese, chocolate, etc., neatly

Place the grater inside a plastic bag and grate in there – *voilà*! The grated food is contained and there's no mess to clean up.

CEEVEE

How to jazz up shop-bought pasta sauce

For cheese sauces: add a couple of sprinkles of dried sage and a tiny pinch of rosemary. For tomato sauces: shake in some chilli flakes (how much depends on how spicy you like your food), add some dried or chopped fresh basil or oregano, and lots of ground black pepper. Top with freshly grated parmesan and a couple of fresh basil leaves.

SARAHFAIRY

If adding fresh ingredients is too time-consuming for you, the easiest trick for tomato-based sauces is to add a few drops of Tabasco and be sure to season well.

LEILU

How to keep asparagus fresh

Lay your asparagus out flat on a couple of paper towels. Place a couple more paper towels on top of the asparagus and roll them up, roly-poly style, making sure that the tips are an inch or so inside the towels. Place in a plastic bag – you can use the one you brought them home in – and they will last for up to two weeks.

SCHERZO9

How to extend the life of fresh herbs

Mix finely chopped herbs with olive oil and freeze in an ice cube tray to use at a later date.

TOOKE

How to keep herbs fresh

Stand them in a large glass of water. Put a small plastic bag over the glass and secure with a tight elastic band. Even difficult herbs, like coriander, will last for a week or more and stay fresh.

PATSHARP

How to make a child's packed lunch interesting

Try letting them help you shop for the food in the supermarket. That way, they get a say in what they eat and what goes into their lunch boxes. Try letting them help prepare their packed lunch. I used to find that having my veggies cut up into interesting shapes made them more interesting. Another top tip is to pop a little note into the lunch box.

ELLE_C_BFFL

When I was little, my mum used to write a message for me on my banana, which my friends and I thought was hilarious!

MARIE5991

How to make roast meat super-tender

Whatever roasting method you use, never cook meat straight from the fridge. A large joint of beef will need at least half an hour at room temperature before going into the oven.

MILOU

How to make perfect meatballs

Perhaps not perfect, but certainly no fuss and super-tasty. Buy a pack of high-quality sausages. Snip at both ends, then squeeze roughly a third of the way down the sausage so that the meat comes away from the casing. Repeat until you have three 'meatballs' from each sausage. Roll them between your hands if you insist on them being perfect, although I find that they come out roughly the right shape anyway.

LEILU

How to minimise the amount of salad dressing you use

Put your dressing in a little spritzer or spray bottle and just use a couple of squirts.

STELLADORE

How to soften butter quickly

Slice the butter thinly and lay out the slices on a plate. It will soften in minutes.

ASILDEM

How to re-heat pizza

Put the leftover pizza in a non-stick frying-pan and heat on a medium to low heat on top of the stove until warm. This keeps the crust crispy – no more soggy microwave pizza.

AWADE

How to ripen avocados

To ripen avocados, put them in a paper bag with ripe apples. The apples give off a gas that causes the avocados to ripen quickly. When just right, keep them in the bottom of the fridge for two or three days if not eating at once.

CANOPUS

How to seed peppers and chillies

When preparing chillies, always wear rubber gloves, especially if you wear contact lenses! Slice them in half and run a knife (away from you) down the chilli. This should remove all seeds easily.

MICHELLE_87

How to slice an onion without crying

This is a verified catering trade secret: just wetting the knife OR the onion should do.

ABI1973

How to coat cookie dough balls in sugar in one fell swoop

Fill a small plastic container with about one cup of sugar, then drop in the cookie dough balls. Swirl them in the container with the lid on, and, *voilà* – all are thoroughly coated in sugar.

CEEVEE

How to improve ANY cookie recipe

Don't just soften the butter, melt it. Gooey to the max. Yum!

TOOKE

How to make a quick crumble topping

Grate the butter (straight from the fridge) with a cheese grater. It's amazing how quickly you can then rub it into your mixture.

BLUMA6914

How to make perfect pastry

For perfect and beautifully light pastry, I substitute a quarter of the plain flour with self-raising. Trust me, it works. Even my mother-in-law liked it and she is a hard woman to please!

KGIRL

How to make scones, buns and cakes come out as light and fluffy as those in the shops

The key is in the handling. Scones can't be over-handled or they become stodgy. Once you have made the dough, touch it as little as possible and only roll out as much as you need. With sponge, air is important. If a recipe wants you to mix butter and sugar, use an electric whisk and whisk the butter by itself first, then add the sugar, and whisk again. When a recipe asks you to add eggs, whisk between adding each one to get more air in. And try not to open the door of the oven a lot – the heat escapes and it causes the baking to compress, making it stodgy.

WSSLAOO

How to stop your potatoes from growing shoots

Put an apple in with your potatoes to discourage the growth of shoots. Also, store them in a cool, dark place in a bag through which they can breathe and this will keep them in good condition.

ELIZABETHEVELYN

How to tell if oil is hot enough for frying

Drop in a single popcorn kernel at the beginning. When the kernel pops, the oil is 180°–190°C/350°–375°F, just the right temperature for deep-frying.

CeeVee

How to make green tea taste better

I always add a little honey to my green tea.

REDLADY

Green tea is typically drunk in mountain countries such as Tibet, Nepal and Ladakh. At heights of 3,000–6,000 metres, water boils at 80°C or less (there is much less oxygen in the air at these heights and the air pressure is considerably lower). Green tea tastes delicious there, and is not at all bitter. It should not be made with boiling water, like the Great British Cuppa, but infused at 80°C like a herbal tea. Just take the kettle off a bit earlier.

CANOPUS

How to steam vegetables when you don't own a steamer

Bring a saucepan of water to the boil. Put your vegetables in a colander and place it on top. Cover with the saucepan lid – *et voilà*!

LEILU

How to keep a microwave clean

Always keep a clean piece of kitchen roll on your
microwave turntable. It will absorb anything that boils
over and can be disposed of and replaced easily.

GILLYANO

How to find the end of a roll of cling film

Use an old (clean) toothbrush and rub it gently along the
roll until you locate the edge. The bristles will help lift
the edge up so you can grab it.

CEEVEE

I always fold over one corner whenever I've used cling
film. Then I just look for that corner. I do this with
packing tape as well.

JILLAROO95

How to get a really good seal on a cast-iron pan

Cast-iron pans need to be seasoned to seal the metal
before use. Wash and dry thoroughly, then coat with
a thin layer of vegetable oil. Place on the top shelf of
an oven at 180°C/350°F/Gas Mark 4 for an hour. Put a
sheet of foil or a baking tray on the bottom shelf to catch
any drips. After an hour, turn off the oven and leave to
cool for several hours. Wipe with a kitchen towel. To
maintain seasoning, use only clear water to wash it and
never put it in the dishwasher.

DAISYMAE

GARDENING

or Therapy via the medium of mud, sweat and tears

How to 'rein in' leggy paperwhites when you're forcing bulbs

> Mix one part rubbing alcohol to ten parts water. Water the paperwhite bulbs with this solution and they'll grow to a nice height, but not that weedy, leggy height that looks disproportionate to the blooms.
>
> CEEVEE

How to choose the best site for a new planting

> Nettles stimulate growth of all other plants and make wonderful compost, so using a site that has had lots of nettles is a good idea.
>
> CALI

How to eliminate couch grass

> Sow turnips where there's a bad infestation of couch grass. It'll look odd, but anything is better than couch.
>
> GAM

How to get hydrangeas to flower blue

Hydrangeas flower blue because of the soil acidity, which is not always naturally the right pH everywhere. The easiest way to ensure a hydrangea flowers blue is to plant it beneath or near a large conifer. The ground will be the right pH because of its neighbouring conifer.

HAPPYCANADIAN

How to get your husband to help you with the gardening

Invest in some serious power tools (a petrol lawn mower and petrol strimmer did it for my husband). He will then feel that they are too powerful for your delicate, lady-like frame (or look like too much fun to miss out on) and volunteer to do it instead! Worked for me.

BURGUNDYORBUST

How to grow herbs

Never plant the same kind of herb in the same place twice in succession.

TROOPS

How to grow *Pieris*

Pieris are hardy shrubs and pretty hard to kill off. The only secret to getting them going is to make sure they're planted in acidic soil. You can get a kit from the garden centre to help you ascertain what type of soil you have in your garden. If it's alkaline, just dig in some ericaceous compost before planting.

ELSIE

How to grow roses

Meat dripping buried beneath a planted rose will make it grow wonderfully.

POLLY

How to improve your vegetable garden

Plant the odd row of French marigolds among vegetables, especially near potatoes and tomatoes, as they kill greenfly.

GRETCHEN

How to revive your chives

You know when chives bolt and get all woody and flowery? Cut them down until they're only an inch or two tall. They should grow back like new.

JANEY93

How to scrape moss off stone easily

Scraping moss off stonework or terracing can be agonisingly hard but it's much easier if the moss is wet. Do it immediately after rain or spray it as you go.

GRETCHEN

How to sow seed successfully

Both seed sowing and transplanting should always be done with a waxing – never a waning – moon. This is scientific fact, not just an old wives' tale.

POLLY

How to speed up composting

You can buy compost accelerator in gardening stores, but this can be pricey. By far the best thing to put into your compost is urine! All those lovely bacteria really speed up the process and are totally free. Now that's what I call recycling!

LADYDIGGER

How to stop pigeons roosting on garden furniture

A fake owl is very successful for deterring pigeons. Put it somewhere visible and near where you want to clear them.

DISTRACTEDHOUSEWIFE

How to stop a water butt from smelling stagnant

Just add some charcoal to the butt – result: no smell.

REDLADY

Cut the foot off a laddered pair of tights and, with a rubber band, fit the foot over the downpipe that feeds the water butt to catch any debris. Every so often, throw the full foot away and put a clean one on.

CTUSSAUD

How to get rid of moles in your garden

If you have moles in your garden, cut open a whole head of fresh garlic, drop it down the hole, cover it up and the mole will move on!

STEPH

How to reduce the number of insects in your garden naturally

Reduce your use of insecticides by creating a pond to attract natural predators, such as frogs. This could be as simple as a small washing up bowl sunk into the ground.

BooBoo

How to save carrots and onions from pests

Plant carrots and onions side by side. For some reason the pests that usually affect them hate this.

JANEY93

How to get rid of ants' nests

Cover the nest in the cheapest talcum powder you can find.

BEKKI007

If they're outside, good old-fashioned boiling water works, although you might have to do it a couple of times.

SEAGULL-PIE

How to eliminate greenfly on roses

Plant garlic next to roses and you will never have greenfly.

GAM

How to deter slugs

This is my latest weapon: slugs hate hair as it sticks to them. Ask at the hairdresser or dog beauty parlour for a bag of cuttings. Spread around your hostas and delphiniums – in fact this would work for any of your plants – and, unless the slugs can pole vault, it should protect your plants.

PATSHARP

How to weed between paving slabs when you have pets and so can't use weed killer

You can pour white vinegar on the weeds to kill them and it will not harm the pets. This works well, but can leave a lingering odour for a day.

MMSTEWART

How to make cut tulips last longer

I bought my mother-in-law a bunch of tulips recently and she put a drop of bleach in the water before she put them in the vase. I couldn't believe it as I thought it would kill them, but it works. I've done it twice now – apparently, it kills the bacteria.

MooBird

How to support tall bushy plants

Use your old wire hanging baskets. Turn them upside-down and let the plant grow through the mesh.

PATSHARP

How to feed houseplants and near-the-house plants

Fill empty milk cartons with water and use the very slightly milky liquid to water any plant before recycling the carton.

TROOPS

How to fertilise houseplants without using weird synthetic chemicals

Epsom salts! Make a solution of two tablespoons of Epsom salts to one gallon of water. Dissolve thoroughly and use the solution to water your houseplants once a month. They'll have lush, gorgeous foliage, and it also encourages flowering plants to bloom more often.

CEEVEE

How to remember to water houseplants

Put a note in your diary or an alarm on your phone.

FUZZYSUGAR

HOME

*or One of the great supernatural phenomena of all time:
where do all the socks go?*

How to successfully swat a fly

A really easy way to swat a fly is to wait until it comes
to rest on something. Get your rolled up magazine
(or weapon of choice) and come at it from the front –
imagine hitting it on the nose. I used to creep up behind
them or directly above, but since I heard that they can
only take off in a forward direction, they fly into the swat
and my success rate has improved dramatically.

TOOKE

How to get rid of spiders when you are arachnophobic

Gather conkers in autumn and place them around your
home under furniture, etc. Or buy 'No More Spiders'
which is a product made from horse chestnut oil, and it
works. We haven't had spiders for two years.

SUPANANA

How to deter wasps

Try hanging a large paper bag with string, tied at the
top, from a tree or the overhang on your porch. Wasps
are very territorial and will not bother you if they think
that there is a larger colony nearby.

AGNES123

How to keep your shaving cream can from rusting and staining the bathroom tiles

Before first use, coat the bottom of the shaving cream can with clear nail polish. This stops moisture from reaching the metal, and therefore stops rust from forming.

CeeVee

How to always have a new rubbish bag ready

Always keep your roll of pedal/swing bin bags in the bin, under the present bag of rubbish, so that when you take it out full, the new ones are at hand underneath.

REDFIFI

How to improvise when you need a low or work table

Most ironing boards have an adjustable height so, when you are short of space, use yours as a table! I sit on the end of my bed and lower mine until it is the right height – good when I need to get my sewing machine out.

Judi

How to keep steel wool rust-free

After you've used the steel wool, pop it in a bag in the freezer. It won't rust and you'll be able to reuse it many times.

GENW

How to open a tight screw-top lid or jar

Run the lid, but not the jar, under hot water – metal expands when heated and allows the jar to open easily. Then use a tea towel to turn the lid.

STAR

How to clean a very dusty room

Use a damp cloth first – the dust will just fly around if you use a dry cloth. Then use a normal polish and duster.

SHAWFIRE

How to clean burnt pots

I add a can of Coke to the pan and boil it. If that fails, a dishwasher tablet left to dissolve in the pan for a while seems to work!

LUCYD

How to clean copper pans naturally

Use ketchup! Spread it on, and let it sit, then wash it off. This works amazingly well on my copper-bottomed pans, which can get really nasty on an electric stove.

JCULL

How to clean lavatory brushes

I found that leaving the loo brush in the lavatory bowl with detergent while I clean the rest of the bathroom cleans it.

LUCYD

How to clean limestone worktops

The porosity makes them prone to staining, even if you've had them sealed. Clean with a mild washing-up liquid solution. Do not use abrasive cleaners or ones containing lemon, vinegar or other acids – they will dull the surface.

BEKSB

How to clean pewter

Try rubbing it with a cabbage leaf. Sounds mad, but it works.

CORKYCHUM

How to clean water stains from marble tops

Try white wine vinegar.

MYSPANDEX

How to fade water marks on antique wood

Mix some table salt with olive oil, to form a paste. Using a cotton cloth, rub some of the paste in a circular motion on the water stain. The salt acts as an irritant, loosening the stain and dirt, while the oil lubricates the wood. Should work beautifully.

MARJORIEUSA

How to find the joy in housework

I make it bearable by putting on some energetic music and dancing around and singing along as I do it. Think of it as a work-out.

BEKSB

How to get rid of cobwebs on high ceilings

Tape a feather duster to a broom – job done with no climbing.

BEKKI007

How to get rid of fish odours in the house

Put a bowl of vinegar in the oven, on a medium heat, to eradicate the smell of fish.

ABI1973

How to get rid of a musty odour in dresser drawers made of plywood

Try sprinkling bicarbonate of soda into the drawers, rub it in, leave to work, and then vacuum out.

MAZCOM

How to get the smell of baby vomit from car upholstery

Sprinkle some bicarbonate of soda over the stain and gently rub it in – it will remove the smell completely. It's inexpensive and works.

INDOGIRL

How to keep silver from tarnishing

Keep a large piece of blackboard chalk alongside it, preferably in a reasonably airtight container. It works by absorbing all the moisture that would otherwise tarnish the silver. Amazing.

PILAR

How to keep the toilet clean

Once a week, drop a denture cleaner tablet into the pan and leave overnight.

REDLADY

How to keep your kitchen sponge from breeding bacteria

Put it in the microwave for a couple of seconds – this kills off the nasties.

DAISYFAY

How to remove candle wax from a painted wall

Put three to four ice cubes in a plastic bag and hold it against the wall for about ninety seconds. Then rub an old credit card downwards on the wax, and it should pop right off.

GDUFFY85

How to remove hairspray from a tiled bathroom floor

Rubbing alcohol (surgical spirit) works best for me. Just wipe on full strength and then wash off.

BEACHY1

How to remove mould from walls

If the walls are painted, there are several solutions. Easiest and cheapest: wash the walls with dilute bleach, then rinse thoroughly and allow to dry. The bleach kills the mould spores. To prevent it returning, make sure the room is well ventilated and paint with a product designed to cope with steamy atmospheres as they contain a mould inhibitor. If it's not a bathroom, then there is a condensation problem and that needs to be addressed to stop it returning. Condensation always goes to the coldest part of the wall.

TRIPLIKATE

How to stack knives in the dishwasher

Always stack knives blade down in the dishwasher so that they can't slash an unwary elbow as it reaches past.

CALI

How to get bubbles out of wallpaper that has dried on the wall

Get a really thin pin and poke it in the bubble, then SLOWLY push out the air using a towel or cloth. Ta da – bubble gone. If you take the air out too quickly, or if you use your fingers, you will end up with a crease.

MADZ

How do you remove mascara stains from carpet

Use a small amount of white spirit on a soft cloth and rub gently – it does work.

REDLADY

How to get matt emulsion paint out of a carpet

Once the stain has dried a little, simply rub nail varnish remover into it with a cloth.

RACHYJAYNE

How to find an inexpensive carpet

Sea grass matting is great, cheap carpet. It's really low maintenance and looks nice for years.

SAMANTHACAMERON

How to get Rawlplugs out of walls

Screw a larger screw into the Rawlplug, then grip it with pliers, and pull in a circular motion.

ALLY1310

How to get your man to put up a shelf

You: 'Can you put the drill on to charge please, sweetie.'
Him: 'Why?'
You: 'I need a shelf putting up and I think it is high
time I started to do these things for myself, darling.'
Him: 'Er . . . You haven't done this before?'
You: 'No, my love, but I hate having to ask you to carry
out these tasks for me.'
Him: 'Don't worry about it. I'll put the shelf up for you.
These drills aren't all that easy to use.'
You: 'Why thank you my angel!'
Just used this ploy and it worked like a dream.

LADYDIGGER

How to paint walls quickly

Forget about using rollers which splash and paint
brushes that you have to keep dipping and wiping in
the paint tray. Get a large car cleaning-type sponge
and cut it in half. Wear rubber gloves and dip it in the
emulsion before lightly 'scrubbing' the wall with it. It
is really, really fast (although you may have to give the
wall another coat when the first is dry). You get two
decorating sponges out of one large sponge and you
simply throw them away afterwards, instead of having
to clean them with loads of water. Just tried this and
painted a huge wall in about three minutes! It was very
even too.

LADYDIGGER

How to hide pesky cables

If you can, get your cables to run along the sides of the walls, and cover them with cheap cord covering material (bias binding is perfect) – they will look far better than black or white plastic. The covering will also protect the cable.

LucyD

How to get stains out of baby clothes

My daughter is now thirteen months old, and none of her clothes have any stains! I swear by Napisan (and I have also worked in a dry cleaner's for the past three years). I have a nappy bucket full of Napisan solution in the bathroom, and at the end of the day I throw my daughter's clothes in there to soak. After two to three days, I throw them in the normal wash on forty degrees and, *voilà*, no stains! I also know that some household cleaners work, but Napisan is anti-bacterial and will not destroy material, and you can use it on anything – plus it's safe for your child.

CharmEB

How to clean a washing machine that has black mould on its rubber seal

Try hot water, lemon juice and a soft toothbrush, then scrub. I also did this for the seal on my fridge.

7THSIN

How to clear holes in a non-stick iron when the instructions say not to use any product in the water chamber

I add some white vinegar to the water and leave it to steam. It does clear the holes.

REDLADY

How to deodorise your washing machine

Fill the detergent dispenser with vinegar and run a
wash cycle on an empty machine. This both cleans
and deodorises the washing machine. It works in the
dishwasher too, AND it removes limescale.

ASHLING

How to fold fitted sheets neatly

Fold the fitted ends in and close them in a drawer – this
is your 'other person'. Then step back and do the same
with the other end, pull sharply, then walk towards the
drawer and put that end in as well. Keep repeating until
it's a neat size – and, *voilà*, a perfectly folded sheet!

ALI161

How to keep a bed linen set together

Keep your matching sets of bedding in one of the
pillowcases. Easy to identify and when you need to
change the bed, everything is together.

PATSHARP

How to get bubblegum out of fabric

Put the item of clothing in the freezer. Once it is frozen,
the bubblegum will peel off quite easily and shouldn't
leave a mark.

MIMI18

How to remove biro from leather

I used hairspray on my leather sofa and it worked very
well. Only spray a little at a time and rub gently with a
damp cloth.

LUCKYWHITE

How to prepare to move house

Here is my big moving tip: when you put stuff in boxes,
label which drawers they come from – such as 'bottom
right kitchen drawer' – not where you're going to put
them in your new home. It makes finding stuff in a sea
of identical brown boxes a lot easier, as you'll remember
where they were in your old place.

BEKKI007

How to transport books when moving house

Instead of creating lots of incredibly heavy boxes full
of books, stack them and tie them with string, like you
would a parcel. Then you have little stacks that aren't too
heavy, which can fit into small spaces and corners when
you're packing the car.

LUDA

How to keep a coal fire going

Keep your old wine corks. One or two thrown on to the
dying embers will definitely perk it up again – like free
firelighters without the smell!

MOTHERKNOWSBEST

How to guard against fire

Never ever leave a paperweight or magnifying glass
where sunlight can shine on it through a window. The
concentrated beam could start a fire in a few minutes.

GAM

HEALTH

or Those magic words I sometimes say to myself: 'OK, you better not go to school today'

How to cure a sore throat with natural ingredients

Chilli is a natural antiseptic that, strange as it may seem, can reduce swelling. A good hot curry, preferably made with fresh chillies, will eliminate a sore throat immediately.

CANOPUS

How to prevent catching the common cold and flu

Wear gloves on public transport – or wash your hands as soon as you arrive, and always use your elbow, never your hands, to open the doors of public lavatories.

CANOPUS

How to deal with cystitis

When I had agonising pain, peeing every three minutes, the best remedy was to sit in a bath of hot water for an hour or two and just pee in the water. It took a lot of the sting away while I waited for the antibiotics to kick in. I know it sounds gross, but try it.

MARILYNPANTO

How to 'de-bloat'

Try fennel tea. It's also great for treating colic.

VENUSO1

How to get rid of embarrassing wind

Peppermint tea. It works wonders. Drink it regularly throughout the day (perhaps substituting it for a couple of cups of tea or coffee), or after you've had a big meal.

KWILKY

How to get rid of trapped wind causing a stomach ache

Even if it's the last thing you feel like, some form of physical activity will help get things moving. If you're in pain or feeling bloated, I recommend lying on your back, knees bent with the soles of your feet on the floor. Keeping your trunk stable, lower both knees together to the left until they touch the floor. Let them rest there for a few seconds. Repeat on your right side. Keep repeating this move for as long as you like, the twisting motion gradually helps relieve the built-up tension. Just make sure you have some privacy as it's likely to make you a bit windy afterwards! Also, at other times, just going for a walk relieves the tightness.

SUNNY2DAY2

How to get more vegetables or fruit into your diet when a) you don't eat any at the moment and b) you really don't like them

Pizza! Buy a thin-crust plain tomato and mozzarella pizza and before you put it in the oven try 'decorating' it with some combinations of vegetables. Ones that work particularly well are mushrooms, sweet corn, onions, peppers, artichoke, small broccoli florets, asparagus, olives, spinach, shredded carrot . . . or anything else you fancy experimenting with. Top it off with some small pineapple chunks if you like. You can get some great flavours this way and it's well-balanced, while still feeling a bit naughty and enjoyable.

SUNNY2DAY2

How to get rid of a mouth ulcer

This sounds weird, but it really does work. My mum taught me this one. Take some icing or other powdered sugar (NOT granulated) and pack it around the ulcer. Do this over one evening, adding sugar as needed. Apparently, it helps the membrane in that area seal and heal itself more quickly. I can now get rid of a mouth ulcer in a couple of days rather than wait a couple of weeks for it to go away on its own.

JILLAROO95

How to heal burns naturally

Aloe vera gel (also called aloe juice) is extracted from the plant's inner leaf and can be used topically to soothe the skin, heal burns and promote cell regeneration.

BETHANY

How to have more energy, I'm always tired

Although it sounds counter-intuitive, the best way to give yourself more energy is to be more active. If you lie in bed eating chocolate all day, you will have virtually zero energy, but if you exercise regularly and eat light meals I promise you'll feel a lot more bouncy. It's the hardest thing in the world to do, but next time you feel like taking a nap, force yourself to go for a walk. Even if you bargain with yourself that if you walk for fifteen minutes then you can have a nap when you get back, I bet you won't feel like napping when the time comes.

NICOLE

How to prepare for a smear test

If you wear a skirt, you can hitch it up rather than take it off, and this can make you feel less exposed. Afterwards, when you hop off the couch you feel dignified immediately, instead of having to find underwear and trousers first.

ROSEBUDSMUMMY

How to stop compulsive hair pulling

I used to pull at my hair all the time when I was embarrassed or flustered. I found that doing something else instead of pulling at my hair helped me to break the habit. For instance, I would tap my fingers or tug on my pocket. Eventually, the habit got less and less frequent and I was able to stop doing things compulsively altogether.

MEVSEVERYONE

How to deal with restless legs

I have had restless legs, and now a restless arm, since I was a teenager. I find that if I take magnesium every day, it's amazing how it disappears after about ten days and only comes back if I stop taking it.

ERMENTRUDE

I find that taking zinc in the morning can help.

GILLMATT

How to soothe a jellyfish sting

When I got multiple jellyfish stings in Mexico, the locals told me to put sand from the beach on the places I'd been stung. It worked surprisingly well, especially as I didn't have vinegar or burn cream, and who wants strangers peeing on you?!

PRINCESSNATA17

How to avoid mosquito bites

Buy some fresh and smelly basil, and put it next to your bed.

ABIUSOFT

How to heal midge bites quickly

I'm a regular camper and always carry Savlon (an antiseptic cream). Before I go to bed at night, I put it on my arms, legs and face so if I get bitten, it works straight away. If you get bites during the day, put it on straight away; it takes the sting right out so you avoid all the scratch marks as well.

SCOTTISHCHIC

How to stop a mosquito bite from itching

Rub a wet bar of soap all over the bite area and leave it to dry – it'll stop it itching!

YVETTE

Several things work: clear nail varnish (yes, it's true!); baking soda mixed with water and smoothed on with your fingertips; banana peel rubbed on the area; or a lemon cut up and gently rubbed on to the bite area. Failing that, you could always go with calamine lotion.

WELSHWONDER

How to deal with mosquitoes

If you dab on Vicks VapoRub, it keeps them away. If you take an antihistamine it stops the itching and helps you sleep. Also, Lanacane cream will anaesthetise the area.

PATSHARP

How to heal post-birth stitches fast

Wheat germ oil is even better than vitamin E oil for healing scars. You can find capsules at health stores: just break them open and apply the oil two to three times a day. It smells a little funny, but is well worth it.

DANIEGENIE

How to deal with cold sores

Use liquorice balm on a daily basis and you won't get any more cold sores.

REDLADY

How to stop drinking the whole bottle of wine when you have one or two glasses but the rest keeps looking at you

Put the cork back in and put the bottle out of sight, then go and brush your teeth. I guarantee you won't fancy the wine then!

MILLI74

How to drink on a night out without getting too wasted

My grandmother had a great idea. She would have one gin and tonic at the beginning of the night, and when anyone asked her if she wanted another, she would say that her current one was a bit strong – could she just have a top-up of tonic in it? She repeated this throughout the evening and everyone always saw her with a full glass, but she'd had only one shot all evening.

ANGIEGW

How to survive hay fever – a cure for runny, itchy eyes and a runny nose

Try to buy local honey. Take a spoonful every day and it will ease your symptoms. Ideally, you should start this before the hay fever season is in full swing, but give it a go anyway.

MOPHEAD

I have endured awful hay fever for years, but recently I've found that the simplest thing works the best: have a shower or bath every night before you go to bed and leave the clothes you've been wearing outside your room (and, preferably, wash them). Throughout the day you pick up pollen on your skin, clothes and hair, so doing this will stop the night-time sneezing fits and you'll hopefully wake up feeling refreshed and non-puffy-eyed.

GEMROSE

How to get to sleep when you find it impossible and have tried every trick in the book

A banana during the hour before bedtime has completely cured my husband who was an insomniac for years.

CANOPUS

How to deal with night sweats

To deal with night sweats and hot flashes specifically, my doctor told me to take soy capsules or eat more things with soy (edamame, soy milk, etc.). He also advised vitamins E and D as well as calcium. It's a bit of a pain to remember to take all of those but, so far, it's really paying off.

STELLADORE

How to gently remove the sticky marks left by HRT patches

WD-40 removes anything sticky.

PATSHARP

How to prepare yourself for your period and cope with exhaustion and cramping

Evening primrose oil is often suggested. I also find taking iron supplements in the week up to and during my period helps. Another sickening, but useful suggestion is light exercise. Hate it, but it does bring relief.

GDUFFY85

How to remember to take your pill every day

If you're working, you normally get up at the same time every day. The first thing most of us do when we wake up is have a morning wee. Keep your pill in the bathroom or where you can spot it while you are having a wee, and the minute you're done, take your pill.

DELSI

How to breastfeed

Before you get into position, make sure you have a pint-glass of water, a large bag of your favourite chocolates, the TV remote and your phone within easy reach as you could be there for hours and it's hard to move once you've started.

ESME

How to cure constipation during pregnancy

Eat a small packet of prunes. You can buy small packs of them to keep in your bag.

BUBBLICIOUS

How to deal with water retention in pregnancy

Eating celery helps, as does drinking more water.

PINKPANTHERJAIME

How to get your partner to understand the irrational, oversensitive behaviour that is commonplace in pregnancy

I think the best way to make him understand is to sit down together when you're NOT feeling like a mentalist (!) and have a laugh about it. Explain to him that the way you are feeling drives you mad too, but it's short-term (you hope!), and his relatively sane partner will be back in the house at some point. Emphasise that any snappishness is not directly aimed at him – he's just the nearest target – but try to explain how fat and unattractive you feel right now. If it provokes a few more compliments and hugs, all the better.

ELSIE

How to stop morning sickness

Eating little and often. I found that starchy foods worked best for me, especially those that take a long time to digest, like porridge. I used to have a bowlful before going to bed at night, as I found I felt less sick when I woke up. Also, ginger is an old remedy – ginger biscuits, ginger beer, or even sucking on a cube of crystallized ginger will all help.

CHICKENLADY

How to inconspicuously refuse alcohol at a staff Christmas party when in the early stages of pregnancy and before you want to tell anyone

Be the driver – that means you can't drink. Problem solved!

DOZIGGY

How to deal with psoriasis

Chickweed worked wonders for my sister! You can infuse the herb yourself or buy it in a cream form to rub in.

ANDREA39

How to treat sunburn

I always burn and have found that Sudocrem (the nappy rash cream) is a miracle worker. Sunburn usually takes days and days to heal, but just slap on some Sudocrem at night and the next morning you'll see a real difference.

BROOKE

Soak a towel or face cloth in white vinegar, diluted with a little cold water, then lay it on the sunburn and it will take the burn out of your skin. I promise this works.

REDLADY

Calamine lotion works a treat, especially if you can keep it in a fridge. And it's really cheap. I've travelled all over Asia and have found it in every country.

CATERINA31

Rub plain yogurt on the area and then leave it to set for half an hour and then wash off. This should make it less red and less painful.

AMELIABELIA

How to get rid of verrucas

I had a verruca for about ten years and none of the medications available worked. I then read about using banana skin. I was slightly dubious, but I tried it and it was absolutely amazing and cleared up my verruca in about a month. Cut a square of banana skin, large enough to cover the verruca, place the fleshy side against the verruca, and keep in place with a normal plaster. You'll notice a difference after twenty-four hours. Change every evening and I swear it works, it's amazing!

GEORGIE137

How to eat whatever you want on a diet

If you eat more slowly and put down your fork between each bite, you'll be more aware of your body and when you're full. And, of course, you absolutely have to exercise.

STELLADORE

How to feel full for longer

Have a big glass of water before you eat. This makes you feel fuller for longer.

xxHazeLxx

How to find calorie-free candy

Stick some grapes in the freezer! They taste sweet and have hardly any calories. Munch a few and you get one of your five a day. Very tasty too.

MINX26

How to stop cravings when on a diet

Keeping busy is key: your mind must be fully occupied and it helps if your body is too. So get deep into something you love that's at least marginally active (telling you to go to the gym would just be cruel). Ideally, get away from the kitchen too. So going shopping is good (who needs to stop for a cake when they're shopping?); watching TV and pottering around the house is bad! If at work with time to spare, perhaps you can throw yourself into tidying your desk, sort your inbox or make a free interactive food log on a site like fitday.com to horrify yourself about how many calories are contained in the things you're craving.

ABI1973

How to improve willpower when on a diet

A picture is worth a thousand words. Take a photo of yourself – from behind – and keep it handy. Every time you are tempted to eat that plate of chips, take a look at that picture.

JILLAROO95

How to lose weight

It's so easy to kid yourself that you don't eat that much and by just looking at a doughnut you put on weight. But we all know that's not true. Keep a food diary (be honest) of what you eat: you'll be amazed how much you do. It's great being slim and anyone who says otherwise is a great big fibber!

ALI161

How to motivate my boyfriend to lose weight

Why don't you suggest that you two have a competition to see who can get the fittest by Christmas/Easter/summer/whenever? Think of a suitably saucy prize for the winner . . .

TOOKE

How to speed up your metabolism

Exercising and taking a cold shower/bath will speed up your metabolism.

TALLULAH

FITNESS

or Fit or fat, the choice is yours

How to remember to do pelvic floor exercises

I do mine every time I'm on the phone to my boyfriend. He doesn't have a clue and I like to think I'm doing him a favour.

SUNNY2DAY2

How to do the hula

When you shake, bend your knees a little – you will see the difference. This is a great love handle squisher!

LEILANIW

How to motivate yourself to exercise

Think of a reason that makes you want to be in shape. I use the fact that I'm going to my best friend's wedding in Maui, where my ex-boyfriend and his new wife will be.

PRINCESSNATA17

How to be motivated to go for a run in the early morning

After you're fairly awake, allow yourself a choice. You can either go for the run, or you can stay at home and go back to sleep. The only catch is you have to stand in front of the mirror, looking yourself in the eye, and say, 'I am giving up on my fitness goal for today because I am too lazy,' or something similar. A big trigger for me is to do the same thing, but in just my sports bra and shorts. That's a big reminder of what you're trying to do.

MISS_ALI1984

How to get motivated to start dieting and working out

Sign up with a friend to do a charity run, like Race for Life in aid of Cancer Research UK, or, if you're a little more ambitious, how about a half marathon? It really helps to get you motivated and you're doing good at the same time. Worked for me.

KEZZ

How to get your husband to diet

Find some healthy eating plans without even saying it's part of a diet. Your husband may start to enjoy the food if he feels better.

ALLY1310

How to ease the pain of sit-ups

Before you start doing sit-ups, lie on your back and curl your knees up to your chest, and hold them. Then slowly release, so your back is in the right position. This makes sure you're doing the sit-ups correctly and improves the effect of them.

PANDSY

How to know when it is best to eat when exercising

It depends on what exercise you are doing. If it is any type of weight training, then eating protein or taking it in the form of a shake should be done as soon as the work-out is finished, and a meal containing protein eaten later on. If it's a cardio work-out, then I would recommend waiting until you feel that your body has returned to a normal pace before eating to avoid indigestion.

PINKPANTHERJAIME

How to get better at the breathing for the front crawl

First, try to slow down your stroke. A common drill that swim teams use is to hold both arms in front, in a streamline position, while kicking. Then stroke with one arm, return it to the front, and stroke with the other – very slowly. As you do this, pay attention to when your elbow comes out of the water on the stroke arm: when the elbow is at its highest, turn your head and start to breathe. As your hand comes forward and your fingers start to dive into the stroke, turn your head back into the pool. Also, be sure to exhale underwater so that you need less time to inhale out of the water.

DEZG

How to avoid foot cramps when swimming

Stretch before and after swimming (yes, stretch your feet!). Try heel raises, flexing/relaxing toes, and make sure your diet has adequate potassium. If you are eating a high-protein diet or working out really hard, there's a chance your diet is low on calcium, magnesium and potassium, all of which are necessary for proper muscle function. So add a good multivitamin or simply eat a banana a day.

DezG

How to make laps go faster when in a pool or on a track

I bought a swiMP3 music player. It is waterproof and it has made swimming much more enjoyable.

MEYMEZ

How to avoid picking up foot infections around swimming pools

The lifeguards wear sandals, so why don't you? I keep a pair of clean flip-flops in my swimming bag that I never wear outside. I put them on in the changing room and wear them out to the pool right until I get into the water. And I wear them in the showers too. I don't take them off until I'm changing out of my bathing suit.

DEWSTER

FRIENDSHIP

*or Cling to the goodies, be ruthless in
dumping the baddies*

How to be just friends with a man who wants a romantic relationship with you

Start treating him like one of the girls. Don't ever dress up around him, just throw on trackies and tie your hair back. Let him see you with unwashed hair and a greasy face. Be casual about it. Give him advice (he'll stop feeling romantic about you straight away), especially about the way he drives or the quickest route somewhere. Talk about your period pains. Ask him to go shopping with you. Ring him up lots for a chat. Invite him round to your place when lots of other people are there and be really friendly to everyone. Pat him on the shoulder. Tell everyone (in front of him) what a great mate he is. Ask him to drive one of your friends home. Don't tidy up your place when he comes round. In short, be super easy and comfortable, and the tension will go. Works like a treat.

INGRIDIBUS

Don't try – you'll only torture him. Let him out of your life so he can get over you.

ABI1973

How to respond when an (unhappily) married friend expresses interest in you

Is he French? If so, this is normal behaviour. If he is British, he needs to be told that you are not interested until there is a lot of clear blue water between him and his divorce.

JOSA2

How to tell a gay friend that you don't like her in that way

You could paraphrase the quote from Jack Nicholson's character in *As Good as It Gets*: 'You know, if that did it for me, I'd be the luckiest girl in the world.'

JILLAROO95

How can I curb my nagging which both my friends and boyfriends complain about

You might start out by wearing a device like a bracelet or some such thing that reminds you to stop and think, 'Will saying this make the situation better?' Every time you are tempted to nag, look at that item and step back mentally.

JILLAROO95

What to do when friends hear you bitching about them

Apologise. Tell them you've had a bad day and even the people you love most are getting on your nerves. Tell them it's about you and not them.

JILLAROO95

How to deal with a friend who constantly texts and uses her phone in your company

Call her from your own phone when you are together and ask if this is the only way you can get to talk to her.

CANOPUS

'Oh, wonderful!' you say. 'You've remembered to bring your mobile! I have some calls to make. I'm sure you won't mind.'

CATINTHEHAT

How to diplomatically get a friend to buy drinks for a change

Order drinks at the bar and just as they're being served, go to the toilet, leaving your friend to pay for the drinks. Works every time.

JAMESJOYCE

How to give honest answers to friends

Tact is key. Friendships are founded on honesty, but you must also be able to gauge correctly how much someone NEEDS to know. 'That's just me, I'm just honest,' is often shorthand for excusing rudeness and cruelty. Your friends must be able to trust you, but there are ways of being tactful and you should make a great effort not to hurt them in the name of your own honesty.

ABI1973

How to react to a friend who keeps letting you down

Why question her behaviour? Look at your own. If she keeps letting you down, why do you believe she'll ever change?

DEZG

How to act when your best friend pushes you away just when her life is falling apart

She may not want to push you away, she may just be testing your friendship. Just be available when she's ready to need you again. Send her a card or note, perhaps something to make her smile, to let her know that you are still her friend and that you still care for her. Around the anniversary of my young son's death, I tend to pull back from my friends, as if testing them, to look after me for a while during a tricky time. We all get through and back on track again after the dodgy dates. Your friend may be pushing you away if everything else is going wrong for her. She may feel she'll hurt you before you hurt her. Be gentle with her.

COLIYTYHE

How to tell someone you love that you think they have a drinking problem

You might start out by obtaining a list of the signs of an alcoholic from your local alcoholism support centre. Or you can find them online. Use this list as the basis for bringing the subject up. Emphasise that you are not judging but worried about someone you love.

JILLAROO95

How to encourage an anorexic girl to eat

The key thing is not to make an issue out of food or eating. Simply forcing the issue will have the opposite effect of what you want to achieve. Has the girl in question sought help? If not, then perhaps she's not ready to admit she has a problem. You should seek professional help from specialist support networks. The key is to boost her confidence, and don't focus on her appearance but on her personality and other unrelated achievements.

APPLEBLOSSOM1985

How to write a letter of comfort to someone who is very ill and you do not know too well

It doesn't really matter what you put – the recipient will just be pleased that you have taken the trouble to write at all. Keep it short and to the point and offer practical help if you want, like dog walking, cooking or whatever would be appropriate.

OPERATIX

How to help a friend through chemotherapy

Often people going through treatment for cancer say they can't concentrate on anything and can't read either. Story tapes or CDs are a great gift. They can listen to them while lying down, without disturbing anyone, and for a while forget about their illness.

PATSHARP

Offer to drive her to appointments, take care of dinner for her (and family if needed), bring over a movie, send funny gifts or flowers, whatever your friend needs that you can provide.

STELLADORE

I'm afraid there may come a time when a little gentle bullying is required too. My dad hated chemo so much that at one point he talked about giving it up. This is where friends and family have to point out just how much the patient is loved and needed. On a practical level, dad always complained of having a horrible taste in his mouth, so a constant supply of jelly babies helped! Chemo can also cause very painful feet – something to do with the way it affects nerve endings – so something as simple as finding a pair of really comfy, thick-soled slippers can be a great help.

LINDACEE

How to be nice to a friend who's given birth

When you go to visit the new baby, be sure to take food. Ideally, pop in at lunchtime and take over the kitchen and prepare something nice while she dozes or nurses the baby. Then look after the baby while she eats.

EUSTON74

I lent my friend ALL my DVDs of movies, TV shows, etc. Six weeks later, after she had had a chance to have some time to herself, I visited again and she and her husband told me that was the BEST gift anyone had given them. They were able to watch them while she was breastfeeding, when they couldn't sleep in the middle of the night, etc. They borrowed them for about three months and really appreciated the thought.

KATE42

How to comfort someone who has just had a miscarriage

For her to recover, it is crucial that she works out her emotions, talks openly about how she feels, and is allowed to grieve. Bottling anything up will only make things worse, and those around her must remember that what she has gone through is both physically and emotionally traumatic. As a friend, you need to be on the lookout for any signs of depression and guilt; and encourage her to seek professional help if these do arise. So be there for her, but focus on letting her talk about how she feels. You can't make it better for her, so sometimes the best you can do is just to listen.

ABI1973

I would suggest that you make a note of the baby's due date and on that day, or near to it, take flowers or send a card to let your friend know that you have not forgotten her lost baby. She will be feeling awful as the time of the baby's due date approaches and it really will be a comfort to know that she is remembered and thought about.

COLIYTYHE

How to refuse to babysit

A foolproof way to decline any sort of contact with a child tactfully is to say you're getting over a cold (you don't have to mention that the cold was actually last year). I've never yet met a parent who had the nerve to persist after that. If you're asked to babysit weeks in the future, say: 'I have tentative plans for then. I'll let you know if they fall through.'

ASILDEM

How to stop a pregnant friend only ever talking about her pregnancy

Being pregnant is a huge thing and is changing her life forever. She's probably very excited and a bit uncertain, and needs her friends to support her. And if you think she talks about being pregnant a lot, wait until she has a child to care for and talk about!

STELLADORE

Tell her that all the hard work, devotion and cost in raising a child culminates in the moment the child looks you in the face, smiles and says those three magical little words: 'I'm leaving home.'

LADYDIGGER

How to help my friend to have the strength to leave her violent boyfriend

I have a friend in the same situation. All you (and I) can do is to be there to support her so that she knows that when she's ready to leave him, she has a great support network around her. Let your friend know your door is always open, and let her talk as openly as she wants without passing judgment, and you will be the first one she contacts when it does happen.

SCOTTISHCHIC

How to tell your best friend you think her partner is cheating

Don't. There is no way you can come out of that situation undamaged and, at the end of the day, it's none of your business. Be there for her if things go tits up, but other than that, leave it.

LINDACEE

RELATIONSHIPS

or All he knows about me is that I'm a good listener

Why the guys we like never call

There are tons of reasons: he's not into you; he doesn't
know you're into him; you're not emotionally available;
he's not looking for a relationship . . . the list is endless.
But don't worry, the one who's supposed to call always
does.

STELLADORE

How to know if he likes you

One word: effort. Does he make an effort to be with you
or to talk to you? Then he's into you.

JILLAROO95

What to do if he doesn't reply to your text message

Do nothing. Respect his privacy. He may be busy or
he may be ignoring you. You'll never know if you send
another text. The second text will only annoy him. And
never let him know that you wasted a single second
waiting for a reply.

MASI

How to find a rich guy

The trouble with going out to find a rich guy is that rich guys have radar for women like that. They will certainly sleep with you, and may well go out with you, but if they know you're after their money, they certainly won't marry you. They didn't get rich by being dumb. There's an old saying: if you marry for money, you earn it twice over. Why don't you just make your own money and look for companionship, humour and love in a man?

WILLA

How to go about meeting a partner on the internet

The profile you create should reflect the real you, not the person you want to be. State what you are looking for without going into what you don't want (it will make you sound too bitter).

JILLAROO95

How to deal with fancying your best friend but you are scared of ruining the friendship by coming on to him

It depends a bit on how old you both are. When older people (who have been around the block a few times!) get together with a friend, it can be hugely successful. Both parties know what they are getting into and have usually weighed up the consequences.

ROSEBUDSMUMMY

How to ask a guy out

You can always buy tickets for a concert or cinema and then invite him, telling him you've been given the tickets. Or have a few friends to drinks or supper and invite him too.

OPERATIX

How to be approachable

When you're out with a group of girls, you might find that guys don't come up to you. Men are scared of groups! If you are out with your girlfriends, head to the bar once in a while on your own to get the drinks. He may well come right over!

LAURICHA

What to do on a first date

The best first date I've heard about was when my best friend was taken to the local theme park. She said it was brilliant as they were doing things and having a laugh and it took away the nerves and awkward silences. Bowling, while cheesy, has the same effect. The cinema is a definite no-no – how can you get to know someone sitting in the dark in silence?

EMU80

How to date

My main test for when I date a man for the first time is to ask myself how much he's discovered about me and how much I've learned about him. I went out with a guy the other week and in the space of two hours, I heard about his schooling, his marriage, his divorce, his kids, his PARENTS' divorce (for God's sake!), his job, his plans for the future . . . I literally couldn't get a word in edgeways, so all he learned about me is that I'm a good listener. There's nothing more attractive than someone who actually wants to know about your thoughts and opinions. But also learn to watch out for the selfish beggars.

LINDACEE

How to get out of a date with someone you find very unattractive without hurting him

Tell him you've been dating someone recently, but it's becoming more serious and you don't think it's appropriate for you to be dating anyone else. 'Sorry to let you down, but I did think it was important to be honest with you.' It's a lie, but it will do the trick without making him feel awful.

TIZZYSMUM

How to refuse a date when you are not interested

Start with a straight, 'Thanks for asking, but I don't think so', because you really don't need to make excuses for yourself. If he asks why, tell him, 'I just don't think we're suited in that way.' If he starts to go on about really liking you, say, 'I appreciate that, but I don't feel the same way, so let's leave it there shall we?' You need to retain control of these conversations. Be firm, but polite, and don't think you have to put up with the guy badgering you. It's not your problem if he refuses to hear the word no.

ELSIE

How to choose between two men

Imagine your life six months, two years, and ten years from now. Assess which man you'd rather be with in each stage of your life. Whoever you see in two or even all three stages of your life, keep.

DEZG

Look at each man's father, assess which one has aged better and how he treats his woman, then choose the man with the best dad.

BOOBOO

A friend once told me, 'Learn to fancy the nice ones – they will make you happy.' Stupidly, I never learned that lesson and as a forty-year-old I am still single (and childless, gulp) because I never fancied the guys who would actually be kind and nice to me. Learn from my mistakes!

TOOKE

How to deal with a man who seems too careful with money

How to deal with him? Accept this part of him because he will not change. Financial habits rarely change. Don't think that anything you do will change his behaviour and don't even try unless you enjoy knocking your head against a brick wall. Financial compatibility is one of the key areas that couples should explore completely before marriage. It's a real relationship killer.

SANDRASIMMONS

How to love

The only answer to this is to love someone as you would want to be loved.

CARISSA

How to stop my boyfriend criticising me – my choice of clothes, lack of fake tan, drinking too much, my family and my friends

The perfect way to make sure he stops criticising everything about you is to dump him!

MENOPAUSALMADAM

How to know if it's normal to have doubts in a relationship

You'll never find the perfect house in the perfect street, facing the right way with the right number of bedrooms. Everything is a compromise and you have to be flexible and adaptable. It can be worked out if you want it to be. It is up to you.

OPERATIX

How to confront a lying boyfriend who hides things from you but insists he's honest

My grandmother used to say that it is easier to shut the door against a thief than against a liar – meaning there is really no defence against them.

Izz

How to successfully argue your point with your boyfriend

If he's drunk, wait until he's sober. If he's tired, wait until he's had some sleep. If he's hungry, wait until he's had some food. If he's generally in a bad mood, just leave him alone until he feels better. Be calm and don't raise your voice. If he talks back, just listen to what he has to say, no matter how stupid it might be. Show him that you heard him: 'I understand that you didn't do that on purpose, but . . .'. Suggest a precise solution: 'You need to start treating me better/You need to be a better man' are not good ones. If it has anything to do with emotions or 'girly' things, put it in very simple words: 'When I put on a dress, it means I want you to tell me I'm beautiful.'

GNRBU

How to make your boyfriend more caring

There's a very wise and true saying: the only thing a woman has ever been able to change in a man is his nappies. If he's not a caring kind of guy, you aren't going to be able to change that. However, you can tell him what you like and what is important to you. If he truly cares about your feelings he will make the effort.

JILLAROO95

How to deal with your boyfriend eyeing up other women

Distract him by making non-sexual observations about the woman he is eyeing up, like, 'That girl has really pretty hair', or 'Great jacket', etc. That tells him you notice he is looking and brings the attention back to you.

WooHoo

You can't stop him looking at other girls any more than he can stop you shopping for shoes you don't need, or spending two hours deciding on what to wear, only to change your mind for the fiftieth time at the last minute. It all comes down to understanding each other. To be honest, he probably doesn't even realise he's looking, it's just one of those built-in, automatic reflex reactions in guys. If, however, he starts comparing you with these other girls, the best way to stop him looking at them is to gouge his eyes out with an ice-cream scoop . . .

BINNY

How to stop the fear of being alone after a long relationship

I suffered from loneliness very badly after my marriage ended. I found myself standing in the street sometimes, unsure of which way to turn as I didn't know what I liked any more, only what 'we' liked. That is the key thing: you have to get to know yourself again. Try and remember what you liked to do before the relationship. Take up an old/new hobby. Buy something frivolous. Ask your friends round. Watch trashy TV that will make you laugh. Find mechanisms that take you out of your slump when you feel the fear coming on. Being alone doesn't have to mean lonely. You'll find a new independence and a lust for the single life again. Unfortunately, just when you are beginning to enjoy it, some guy will come along to ruin all your fun!

DEEDEE73

How to know if he is cheating on you

Mine started wearing purple silk boxer shorts. I can only assume it is a ritual for guys afflicted with Wandering Willy syndrome . . . a need (if you will) to decorate the appendage in imperial purple. By the way, I found that the placement of a hidden voice-activated dictation machine within the confines of the car offered a good deal of information.

LADYDIGGER

How to play it if you know your boyfriend is a cheater but cannot tell him you found out. How to get revenge and move on

Be classy. You don't have to tell him you know he was cheating on you in order to get revenge. In fact, the most effective way of hurting him would be to dump him on the pretence that he's too dull/you're just not very attracted to him any more/you don't think he's real long-term partner potential. He knows he's a cheating scumbag, and he'll also think that you're dumping him on the simple basis that in some way he is completely inadequate.

CATERIANNE

How to respond to an anonymous text telling me my boyfriend is cheating, but he is denying it

Get HIM to call the number back, in front of you (especially if he does it from his phone). If he cares about you, there's no way he could back out of it.

TOOKE

How to ask the friend you have been sleeping with for a commitment

You aren't friends; friends don't sleep together. Friends go out for coffee, chill out, etc., they don't have sex! Only sleep with someone who is committed to you – don't give yourself away for nothing.

DOZIGGY

How to have a relationship with a commitment-phobic man

Some women go for men like this because subconsciously they themselves don't want to be tied down. If you enjoy hard work with very little reward at the end of it, go for it!

LINDACEE

How to find great conversations with my boyfriend without boring one another

Take up a new hobby together – the more outlandish the better. That will give you a host of things to talk about.

JILLAROO95

How to get him to talk more

Go for long drives. Men seem to talk more when you are sitting shoulder to shoulder and not face to face. I think they get intimidated by the eye-contact thing. Steer the conversation away from relationships on the first few drives.

MASI

How to make a man listen to you

Go over to the television, switch it off, stand in front of it and say what you want to say!

MENOPAUSALMADAM

How to encourage your boyfriend to tidy more

Make a boyfriend box. Use a storage box and tell him that you are going to fill it with any of his things that you find out of place. If he doesn't reclaim them by the time the box is full, you will sell/donate/chuck the contents of the box.

LITTLEMISSSUNSHINE

How to deal with a guy who's promised to break up with his girlfriend to be with you but never does

I don't mean to sound harsh, but he isn't going to leave her. If he really wanted to he would have done it already. He just wants his bread buttered on both sides. Besides, what's to say he won't do the same thing to you?

RENCHA

How to stop being scared of dating

Pretty much everyone is nervous when it comes to dating. Try to look on it as an adventure – tell yourself that it's exciting, not scary.

JILLAROO95

How to act around your ex when you are still friends but he is finding it hard to move on

You have to realise that when a relationship is over, the perks of being a friend are over. You have to go cold turkey, at least until BOTH of you are over it and want to be friends again.

LAZZYKITTYY

How to act when you find dirty texts sent to your boyfriend's phone from his ex

You need to make it very clear to your boyfriend that you will not be happy if he is still in regular contact with this woman. His ego is currently getting a good old massage and he's only going to cut ties with her when it hits home what he's at risk of losing. I've no doubt she means absolutely nothing to him, but he must feel like sex on legs at the moment and what man is going to knock that back until he's forced to?

LINDACEE

How to deal with an ex who says he misses you but hasn't told you he has a girlfriend

Tell him you miss him too, and that you were only saying that last night to your new boyfriend . . .

LADYDIGGER

How to deal with finding naked photos of your partner's ex-wife among his belongings

Don't you have old love letters? A few photos of your exes? Yearbooks with hearts drawn around the boys you liked? All of those things can be less shocking than naked photos but they all mean the same thing: we like to document our history. Those naked photos are a part of your partner's past. Stop looking through his stuff (yes, we all deserve to have something private).

STELLADORE

How to deal with your ex taking the kids out for the day with his new girlfriend

Accept that your ex was always going to meet someone new at some point and, providing you trust him to look after your kids properly, look on these excursions as an opportunity for you to have some grown-up time for yourself. Arrange to see your friends, go for a beauty treatment, go clothes shopping, go to the cinema to see something non-cartoonish (!) or, when you're a little more chilled about the situation and don't need the distraction, just enjoy a little time alone. I'm sure you agree that your ex has every right to see his kids, and his present/future girlfriends will never mean anything to them in comparison to you, so spin something positive out of these occasions.

ELSIE

How to get over an ex

Treat yourself like a recovering addict – you are addicted to this man and you need to wean yourself off him. You can only take things one day at a time. Say to yourself: 'Today I will not contact him.'

TOOKE

How to be gracious when he doesn't bother with your first wedding anniversary

Tease him about it. This way you can get your point across without any aggro. He will be feeling guilty anyway. Teasing and joking seem much the best way to deal with any grievances, actually.

OPERATIX

How to keep a post-birth marriage happy

Take time to talk to each other – take time over dinner at a table, face to face, and ask how he is, how he is finding the new routine, and try to remain interested in his work and what he does all day. Though it might be the last thing on your mind, your love life is vitally important too. So mentally put aside time for romance: I say mentally, because at this stage spontaneity doesn't come naturally, so, without telling him, add it to the routine you are probably doggedly following (awful as it sounds, it helps to schedule it in!). Even better, do something special for him on a week night, when he's least expecting it.

ABI1973

How to maintain your relationship after giving birth

Don't forget each other as you'll both be showing massive amounts of adoration to the new arrival and either partner can get jealous of that. Make sure you say, 'Thank YOU for our baby,' so your partner knows he's responsible for your happiness.

ESME

How to find out if a man is married and hasn't told you

Listen to your inner voice and what it is telling you. Other signs: a white tan line on his ring finger; he won't give you his home phone number; he doesn't introduce you to family members or close friends; he cancels dates often and at the last minute; he is never available for overnights or weekends away; and he never talks about his home life. Just a few thoughts.

ASHLING

How to get over the fact that you have to share him with her and their kids

You don't have to. No one is forced to do/accept anything they don't like. We all have a choice. What I am going to tell you now is the best advice I have been given and it really worked for me: make a decision, stick to it, don't look back.

MILOU

How to discipline your boyfriend's child without causing conflict when you live together

My advice would be to leave the disciplining to your boyfriend and not get involved. However, that doesn't mean accepting bad behaviour. When the child is behaving badly, gently point out that he needs to deal with it. Men are often unaware so a gentle 'Jimmy is peeing in the sink, can you sort it out?' will prompt him to deal with it. Build the relationship slowly with the child. My daughter adores her stepfather but he took it slowly and sat back and let her learn to love him.

ERMENTRUDE

How to face somebody every day who has turned you down without feeling utterly awful

Turn it around: if a guy you didn't fancy asked you out and you turned him down, would you expect him to avoid you? I doubt it. I'm sure he's also slightly embarrassed, but the best thing you can do is brazen it out. Smile and say good morning next time you see him and get on with your day.

ELSIE

How to keep a relationship interesting and exciting

(1) Write him Post-it notes and stick them in places where he'll find them when you're not there. (2) Establish a fortnightly date night, where you alternate who chooses the restaurant/movie, and keep it a surprise until you get there. (3) Find fun things you can do together, ideally in the comfort of your own home (where you're most likely to stick to them!). This means anything from inventing your own cocktails and naming them, to playing Monopoly. (4) Give each other space! Nothing will kill the romance like spending too much time together. Just think: if you spent all your time together, you'd never have any funny stories to share. (5) Keep the passion by surprising each other. Think massages, naked twister, chocolate sauce fights or whatever. Just remember to keep things spontaneous.

CATERIANNE

How to deal with dating a guy you get on well with but whose kissing you don't like

Several ways: you can either stick to your guns and hope he adjusts to you, or you adjust to him. Guys love it if you say they're good at something as it boosts their self-esteem, but be subtle and say, 'I love the way you kiss but it turns me on more if you . . . [describe how you want him to do it]'. And if he knows he's satisfying you, he will do it more.

BOOBOO

How to know if he just wants sex

Suggest going out on a proper date. If he says something like, 'I'd rather come round to yours to watch a DVD or something', feel free to interpret that as, 'I have no intention of spending any money on you, having my mates see me with you, or listening to you any more than I have to – I just want sex with you.'

TIZZYSMUM

How to ask your boyfriend when you want sex

Depends on the guy – here are a few suggestions:
(1) The stealth mode (guys use this a lot): start out by giving him a back-rub or otherwise caressing him and ending up with your hands under his shirt, and progress from there. He'll get the message.
(2) Bring it up in a flirty/joking way. This will break the ice and make you both more comfortable.
(3) Be direct, as in 'I'd really like to _____.'
(4) Grab him by the lapels and throw him on the bed or other horizontal surface. Unless he has power issues, he'll be extremely flattered and turned on.

JILLAROO95

How to be good in bed

General rules for a good time in the sack include the following:

– be relaxed

– make him laugh (try a seductive dance wearing only his socks and a tea towel!)

– NEVER discuss your past amours in bed

– feel great about your body. He already feels that way about your body, otherwise you wouldn't be in bed with him. Your personal confidence will make you feel and look fabulous

– treat his body like an adventure. Tell him how attractive he is

– in short, massage his body AND ego and he will be gagging for more.

LADYDIGGER

Stop watching movie sex – it's not real! The real thing is silly, messy and fun, and not perfect every time. So one day it might be great, the next, for whatever reason, just OK. Show willing, it's a real turn-on. Don't put pressure on yourself to try a million different things because you're worried the missionary position is boring. Just ask what he likes and say what you'd like in return! Now stop reading this, and go practise, practise, practise!

DEEDEE73

NEVER fake an orgasm! First of all, it's lying to your partner, and if it's more than just rolling in the hay, that's never a good idea. Secondly, if you respond favourably to something that he's doing, he's likely to keep doing it. So you're encouraging him to do whatever random not-good thing he happens to be doing at the time.

GUAMAE

How to sleep next to a guy in a sexy way

Just wanted to share the sexiest thing my man said to me in the first month of dating . . . 'As much as I love you getting dressed up to the nines and looking glamorous, the most intimate boost to my ego is seeing you first thing the morning after, with no make-up and bleary eyes, because no one else gets that chance to wake up with you but me.' Yeah, I love him.

HEROINEGIRL

How to stop an unhealthy relationship

Have a good think about why you've stayed with him so far. Are you so horrible a person that he's all you deserve? Do your friends think about you in that way? I bet they don't. Talk to your friends about why you feel you deserve this treatment. Whether you accept it or not, you definitely deserve better and will probably look back on this episode and wonder why on earth you stayed with him as long as you did!

TizzysMum

Here is a good mantra for life, and not just men. I often give it to my divorce clients: 'You can only – ever – control your own actions, not those of anybody else, so don't waste your time trying.' This man will mistreat you as long as you let him, so stop letting him.

CORKYCHUM

How can I end the relationship with my three-year-old son's father without it hurting my son

Never speak ill of his father to your son. If your son tells you that his dad says bad things about you, tell him that his daddy is feeling unhappy, and that if he (the son) tells his father that he loves him, it will help. Tell him that no matter how his father feels about you, he loves the son. If the father is a total pill, your son will figure it out on his own when he's older, and you will have taken the high road.

ASILDEM

How to get over being dumped by your husband of forty-two years

Tell yourself that you are moving on to a new phase of your life, one that is open to many possibilities. (I know this is hard now, but it will get easier as time goes by. In the meantime, make it your mantra.) You have the chance to redefine who you are and live your life on YOUR terms. You might also want to concentrate on those things your husband did that got on your nerves, and be thankful you no longer have to deal with them.

JILLAROO95

How to believe 'I'm worth more than this' when a man is not treating you well

Ask yourself, very seriously, what you would think/feel/say if your best friend had such a relationship? Or your sister? Or daughter? Are you worth less than these people?

JENNYNIB

How to get my boyfriend to let me go

You should be making the decision to move on. Don't give him the power or control, this is your decision. Presuming he's not a stalker and doesn't have you tied up in a basement somewhere (with a copy of this book, of course), all you have to do is walk away and not look back. A clean break is often the easiest: don't talk, call, text, etc. Set YOURSELF free.

DezG

A kissing tip for men

Just occasionally, enjoy kissing for its own sake and don't assume that it's a prelude to sex. There's nothing more tiresome than being mid-snog and just KNOWING that he is, without fail, going to make a grab for your boob.

LindaCee

WEDDINGS

or It's not about the day, it's about the days after

How to keep your mother under control when planning your wedding

First of all, you have to remember that she has probably been thinking about this day (on and off) since the day you were born. OK, so it's YOUR day and everything, but have a little compassion for the woman who looked after you for all those years. (It'll also be kinda weird for her to see her baby all grown-up and married, and she may be facing some 'I'm-getting-old' issues of her own.) So try to include her in as much as you can, and perhaps give her certain jobs of her own (not just the boring ones) so she can really feel she's had some input. She's probably not trying to take over, she probably just wants to feel included.

REGINA

How to set a wedding date

Before you name the day, look at any potential sporting fixtures or any other major events that may be happening on dates you are considering.

FLAVIA

How to get a good price on your engagement ring

Do your research! Spend a little time on the web researching and comparing prices – bluenile.com is a good place to start. That way, you can see how much you should be paying for a certain size and type of stone. Then, when you go to the jewellery store, you'll be in a much stronger position to bargain. Also, if you avoid the big chain jewellery shops and look for independents and boutiques, you are far more likely to get a discount (up to thirty per cent), as they know that people tend to return to the place they bought their engagement rings.

BRITTANY

How to have a great wedding day

Plan it so that on the actual day of your wedding, you have nothing to do apart from getting ready, and no one is expecting you to write place cards or do anything else. You should give yourself that one day.

ROWENA

How to relax about your boyfriend's pending bachelor party

Just make sure you have a FAB hen night and don't worry about what he is getting up to. Being obsessed and questioning him is a sure turn-off and will make him not want to talk to you about stuff. Enjoy your night out and let him enjoy his!

DOZIGGY

How to plan for a wedding in hot weather (especially for brides who get sweaty when nervous!)

On my wedding day, with my hair up and make-up done, I stripped off and sat in an ice-cold bath for twenty minutes before getting dressed and rocking down the aisle. I had heard that Paula Radcliffe did this after training as it cooled her body right down and lasted for ages. It worked a treat and I got through a whole hour in a packed church during the scariest moment of my life without breaking as much as one bead of sweat. That made my wedding day. I had been so scared about how unattractive a sweaty bride would look. This is the answer: it may not be comfortable but it works and since then, for any potentially hot and uncomfortable occasion where looking good and cool is key . . . on goes the cold bath!

AMBER

How a bridesmaid can really help out before the big day

Offer to run errands for the bride, or even be her chauffeur for the day. There are always so many little things to be done and using public transport makes them twice as hard.

NOREEN

How to be aware of the most important 'bridesmaidly' duty

Helping your friend go to the bathroom if she's wearing an enormous dress is it! Someone else can do pretty much everything else, but if the dress is bigger than the toilet, she's going to need some pretty intimate help.

KAITLYN

How to thank younger bridesmaids on your wedding day

Make up some of your own goodie bags. They'll be less expensive and more personal than buying something ready-made. Fill little fabric bags with toys, sweets, and games for them to play with during the day. With a larger budget, add a bigger gift, which they can keep as a present for being your bridesmaid.

LARISSA

How to have eco-friendly, cheap confetti

Remove rose petals from the flowers before they open and store in a container in the freezer. On the day of the wedding, take them out and either leave natural or spray with a scent.

MARINA

How to negotiate a fair price for corkage

Do this before you make the booking for the venue. If you make it clear that the booking depends on how negotiable they are, you might be able to get a good deal. Speak to someone senior who has the authority to make a decision. Be willing to compromise, too. If they're not willing to reduce corkage, find out what else they can do.

ROOI_SKOENE

How to save money on your wedding

Ask your local horticultural college if they have students who could do your flowers, or ask a member of staff at a florist if they do private work – be discreet about this though. Have only two courses for your meal. Look for your dress in the sales. Ask your local Women's Institute or catering college if anyone can make your cake, or buy an iced fruit or sponge cake and decorate it yourself.

COLIYTYHE

Use eBay for napkins and place cards, etc., to match your chosen colour scheme. It's usually much cheaper than having printed cards done. If you know someone who has lovely writing, you could ask them to write out the place cards. You can print off your own invitations using clip-art and some nice coloured card. Venues are often cheaper midweek than at weekends.

COLIYTYHE

People tend to overspend on flowers. In the church, you really need only two arrangements either side of the altar. That is where people will be looking, and most churches are beautiful enough without flowers all up the aisles. You should also look into whether anyone else is getting married in your church on the same day, so you can all share the cost. Make the arrangements dramatic by having lots of foliage, but with enough large, white flowers for contrast.

JOAN

Definitely get friends to drive you to and from your wedding and reception. I was driven to the church by one of my parents' best friends (lovely for them and me) and went away in my husband's own car (a clapped-out banger covered in foam and tin cans), driven by a non-drinking friend in a borrowed chauffeur's cap. It was more meaningful for all of us, the guests got it and it cost nothing.

ESME

I once went to a wedding party in a pub, with a hilarious personalised pub quiz instead of dinner. It was probably a lot cheaper than most, but we all loved it and stayed long after the bride and groom had left!

LIBBYUK2003

There is absolutely no shame in asking for donations towards your honeymoon instead of a present. And your honeymoon doesn't have to be expensive: a long weekend in Paris (and then returning home quietly and taking the phone off the hook for a week!) could be just as romantic and memorable as a two-week safari – and, in any case, all you'll want to do is sleep, so don't plan anything too busy.

ABCHIS

How to figure out where to go on honeymoon on a budget

Look closer to home. Stop and ask yourself what you want from a honeymoon. Is it adventure and exploration, or just a week in bed with your new hubby and wine? If it's the latter, renting a cottage in another part of the country could be a cheaper option, with much less hassle. Who says a big bed and a log fire isn't as romantic as sun, sea and sand?

GDUFFY85

How to ensure perfect wedding photos

I have been to a few weddings recently where there were one or two of those disposable cameras on each table at the reception. While the professional photos were being taken, many guests amused themselves by taking candid shots of each other, the minister having a wee drink, the kids up to no good, etc. The cameras were later gathered up at the end of the evening by an usher and developed.

MENOPAUSALMADAM

How to find a great wedding photographer without getting ripped off

Ask your local college/university if any of their final year photography students do private work.

AHLH

How to incorporate the 'something borrowed' into your wedding outfit

Need to add a 'something borrowed' into your wedding ensemble but don't want to spoil your look? How about grabbing a quick squirt of one of your mum's perfumes on your way out? That way you don't end up wearing that dodgy necklace/ bracelet/ring that a well-meaning family member has foisted on you, but that doesn't match your chosen 'look'. Simple.

FIONAB

How to incorporate the 'something blue' into your wedding outfit

Traditionally, the bride wears a garter with a blue ribbon or has a blue ribbon stitched inside her dress. You can be much more inventive, though, by wearing: a piece of jewellery with a blue stone; blue nail polish (best for the toes!); blue lingerie; blue make-up (eye shadow, glitter, eyeliner or mascara); little blue handbag to keep lipstick and tissues to hand; or a blue-trimmed hankie just in case! Alternatively, how about some blue flowers or blue ribbon in your bouquet, or blue confetti.

TEGAN

PARENTING – THE EARLY YEARS

or Damage limitation

How to be relaxed with your first baby

Try to leave the baby alone with someone else within the first few days, so it doesn't become something you and your partner start to fear. As much as the baby has to get used to being with someone else, you have to get used to it too.

ESME

How to survive with a brand new baby

In the first days after the birth, lots of people will want to visit. It's your partner's job to keep unwanted visitors away and to do so with diplomacy. Remember, everyone has good intentions so treat them with kindness but be firm. You are likely to be exhausted and will want to have lots of quiet time to bond with your baby and get used to the new routine. At the same time, do not shun close relatives whom you want to feel involved, and don't be shy to ask friends to help you with household chores, such as loading the dishwasher or just making a cup of tea, when they do come. You will literally have your hands full.

JOANG

How to calm a crying baby

A crying baby is often calmed by being held across your tummy and having his or her bottom patted to the rhythm of a beating heart. At the last stages before birth, their bottoms sit just under your heart, so mimicking this is very reassuring to them.

EMERALD

Try swaddling the baby in a blanket; they often don't like their arms and legs being able to wave around too much. It makes them feel more secure.

BEKKI007

You need to go through the checklist first. Changing, feeding, too hot or too cold. Putting them in a warm bath sometimes does the trick, and babies love to be massaged, just as we do. Use some baby oil and put baby on your lap on a big towel, dim the lights and gently massage away. If all this fails, a drive in the car seems to work. It passes . . .

PATSHARP

How to remove cradle cap

Gently massage your baby's head using a soft-bristle baby hairbrush while washing the hair with his or her regular shampoo. It doesn't hurt your baby and is very effective in removing cradle cap.

WELSHLASS

Use breast milk. It's naturally healing.

M

For babies, the only thing midwives recommend is extra virgin olive oil. However, Vaseline works even faster. Best of all, is a mix of Vaseline and Sudocrem (to aid healing), applied throughout the day and slathered on thick at night (make sure your baby is well swaddled so that he or she doesn't rub or scratch it all off). Use this mix to treat cradle cap – it should clear up in a matter of days, depending on how bad the case – then switch back to olive oil. Vaseline is not a good long-term solution, as it simply locks in moisture and doesn't actively moisturise the scalp.

ABI1973

How to keep your baby changing area clean

If you suspect your baby has a seriously dirty nappy, place a clean nappy underneath his or her bottom, before taking the old one off.

ESME

How to calm a screaming two- or three-year-old

I often used this with my little Montessori pupils, with great success. Get down to their eye level and speak to them in a very low, calm voice. They have to stop screaming to hear what you say and they usually do.

ASHLING

How to calm babies or toddlers down

While I was pregnant, I put a favourite soothing tune on my mobile phone, and then, when sitting down or resting, I played the music to my bump. After I had my son, whenever he got stressed out or upset, I played that music to him, and, hey presto, he calmed right down.

NZROCKS

How to cope with a toddler's tantrum

Apparently, we all need to be understood – studies have shown that if you mirror a toddler's words and feelings in a calm voice (even if it feels silly), it shows that you 'get it' and it calms them down.

TWINK

How to keep your toddler's socks on

All toddlers like to remove their socks in a concerted campaign to lose them and cause hypothermia. Put thick tights on them instead and trousers over the top, and their sock removal activities will be at an end. This works very well on my two-and-a-half-year-old son.

MALCOLM

How to convince a toddler to brush his teeth properly

I used to child-mind for two wonderful little boys who weren't that keen on brushing their teeth, so I made it into a competition: who could get the sparkliest teeth. They would rush to the bathroom, brush, come dashing back to show me, and I would pretend to be blinded by their teeth, shining like pearls, and cover my eyes and fall back on the couch. They would shriek with laughter and the winner would get to pick their bedtime story; every night was a draw so they got a story each.

VALENTINE

How to get your children to use dental floss

My son's gums were bleeding after he'd just brushed his teeth, so I asked him if he'd been diligent about flossing. When he said no, I said, 'Wouldn't it worry you if there were blood coming out of your eyes, ears or nose?' He was sort of horrified by this vivid picture and has been flossing ever since.

CEEVEE

How to get your seven-month-old baby to sleep through the night

My baby kept waking because he was rolling over and getting stuck on his tummy when he slept in a baby sleeping bag. His dad tucked him in very tight with a blanket and now he sleeps right through.

EUSTON74

How to get a baby/child to sleep

I bought a 'white noise' CD which worked. It works for exhausted parents, too!

SKI1970

How to stop your two-and-a-half-year-old daughter getting out of bed repeatedly every evening

Just put her straight back to bed. Don't talk to her or acknowledge her, just put her back in bed. She'll soon get the message.

BEKKI007

How to get a three-year-old to sleep past 6 a.m., no matter what time he goes to bed

Get a cute alarm clock and set it together every night, so your child knows what time is getting-up time. If he or she wakes up before it goes off, they will know it's not getting-up time yet, so they can look at a book or play with a toy until it goes off. Worked a treat with my niece and nephew.

BEANO

Very difficult. You can try making sure that no light gets past his curtains. After that, manipulating the alarm clock is the best way. On the first morning, set the alarm for ten minutes before he usually wakes up. When it goes off, go straight in and make a big fuss of him for staying in bed until the alarm sounded. After that, move the alarm clock on by five minutes each day, and within ten days or so, you should be able to get him to stay in his room until a reasonable hour.

ROSEBUDSMUMMY

How to get your child to listen to a bedtime story

Children want to be engaged with their parents; it gives them security. So, while reading to your children, engage them in conversation about the book, asking open-ended questions. If a character in the book says or does something, ask the child what he thinks the character was thinking or feeling. You can learn a lot about what your child is thinking and feeling by listening to his answers, plus you are building his conversational skills and preventing the development of test anxiety by getting him used to answering non-threatening questions. End every day with cosy snuggle/reading time with Mum/Dad, tender talks, and lots of love.

ASILDEM

How to help children sleep in unfamiliar hotel rooms

I purchase a bunch of inexpensive glow sticks (from camping stores) which they crack alight. They have fun playing with them before bed and the security of a safe, glowing light if they wake during the night. If your child is under three, or inclined to chew things, you could hang them on something out of reach during sleep time. The gentle light will last all night.

SARAIO

How to toilet-train a two-year-old who won't use a potty

All two-year-olds will work for something: Smarties, small toys, raisins, etc. Do a deal and offer rewards. Start small, with a reward for agreeing to sit on the potty. Then introduce rewards for performing, etc. The ultimate reward is being free of nappies and having real pants or knickers! Big celebration!

HELENCLARKJAMES

Two years old is still quite young so it could be that he or she isn't ready yet. Things that worked for me included taking her to the loo with me every time I went and describing what I was doing, plus never getting cross when accidents happened (essential, but a tall order!). However, the best tip is to buy pants with a favourite character, such as Thomas the Tank Engine, etc. They will be thrilled and will not want to get Thomas dirty/wet!

VAUNIEATHOME

Two-year-olds can be very strong-willed, and if potty training is a control issue, you must pretend that it doesn't matter to you. Give the child the illusion of control, and make him feel he is choosing to use the potty. Mix in lots of hugs, praise, and unconditional love. And always remember: this too will pass. No child ever went to university carrying a diaper bag.

ASILDEM

How to get a child to eat

If you have a friend with a child who is a good eater, invite them round for meals. Often, when children see others eating without a fuss, they start to do the same.

LENCKE

I've always had set meal times at the dinner table. I serve ONE meal and the kids either eat it or starve until the next meal goes down. I don't serve anything I know a particular child really hates, but I also don't indulge faddy eating. If the child is hungry, it will eat; if not, that's fine. No shouting, no big scene. Children clear the table and that's it until the next meal is served. Absolutely no eating between meals. Never once did any of the children's pals come to my house and not tuck in with the rest of us. I did, however, have amazed mothers saying things like, 'How on earth did you get him to eat that?'

NUMPTIEHEID

Turn it into an apparent carefree game that kids won't see through, such as who can crunch carrots/cucumber/celery the loudest?

JOANG

Have a painting session, then offer a prize to any child who can find and eat foods (from a selection you have to hand) of each of the colours used in their artwork: red strawberries, blueberries, green grapes, yellow banana, etc.

EMERALD

Have them 'Sing a Rainbow' and then 'Eat a Rainbow', as recommended by chefs. Have a picture of a rainbow on the fridge and offer your child a sticker for every shade of food he or she eats.

ESME

Children are less likely to notice whole grains in toasted, rather than untoasted, bread.

ABI1973

How to get children to eat vegetables

Make the vegetables into a funny face pattern on the plate. For example: sprouts for eyes, carrot nose and peas lined up for a smiley mouth. I found this did the trick and works really well with fruit as well.

LOULOUGIRL

My friend puréed vegetables and mixed the purée with pasta sauce. Her son ate the meal and developed a tremendous liking for vegetables.

PATTIEDOG

How to get your children to eat fruit

Try having a colour day. Tell your children you will only eat red vegetables and fruit on a certain day and see what they come up with.

RACHAELICIOUS

What to do for your children's birthday parties

We had a great 'junk party'. Friends saved cereal boxes, big boxes, loo rolls, everything. We hired the church hall, set up tables with glue, paint, glitter and let the kids make whatever models they fancied. They had a fantastic time and took their models home with them. Just remember to tell them to come in old clothes!

PENE

How to get sand out of a child's eye

Get the child to look up, with his head tilted to the side and the problem eye nearest to you. Then slowly pour water from a jug into the eye beside the nose. The water will run across the eye, down the face and on to the floor (so a bathroom, or a tub is recommended). This should clear all the sand after a few jugs.

BEKKI007

How to entertain two kids, aged five and seven, cheaply

Go on a nature walk and make them look out for different bugs and trees on the way. They could take wax crayons and make tree rubbings too.

FRUITYLOOP

Do you bake, even a little bit? Make a cake with them. Sure, you'll have a disaster to clean up in your kitchen, but kids love to cook and are seldom allowed to do most of the steps by themselves. Cakes don't require knives so they could do it all. Then they could take the cake to someone who is ill, or even just a neighbour.

STELLADORE

How to have stylish kids

Let them wear what they want (assuming that it's appropriate for the occasion). Making them style-conscious at a young age will only make them more materialistic and shallow when they grow up. Some of the happiest memories of my childhood did not include worrying about fashion or what I looked like. Now grown up, I worry about them a considerable amount (without pressure from my mother).

S123

How to help children get through the fear of an injection

I've found it helpful to tell my kids to turn their heads away from the arm getting the injection while blowing out hard, as though blowing out a candle. The distraction of blowing out helps tremendously (I even do it myself!).

CeeVee

How to keep your home tidy with kids

Having plenty of storage is the first thing. Make a game of tidying up. This works even for the smallest child. Set a timer for, say, three minutes and have a race to see who can tidy up the fastest. Have a Put-things-back-before-you-take-a-new-thing-out rule. Have a periodic clear-out of broken toys and games they have grown out of.

ASHLING

How to make great play dough

I love this recipe. It doesn't dry out unless you're actively trying to do so!

1 cup flour, 1 cup warm water, 2 teaspoons cream of tartar, 1 teaspoon oil, $\frac{1}{4}$ cup salt. Mix all the ingredients and stir over a medium heat until the dough ball is not gloopy. After it has cooled, colour the dough with food colouring.

AGNES123

How to not lose a child while out

My mother used to dress my brother and me in very bright matching clothes when travelling. This meant that we could generally spot each other in a crowd. Not great for your street cred to have a younger sibling in the same get-up as you, but hey!

LUCYD

How to stop little boys fighting

Have a long chat about why people go to war. They won't understand a word, but will be so bored they will stop fighting.

TOOKE

How to not swear in front of children

Find words that are as close as possible to what you are trying not to say, without sounding too much like them. For example: 'oh my goodness' instead of 'oh my God'; 'blimey' instead of 'bloody'; 'cripes' instead of 'cr*p'; and 'bother' instead of 'b*@?!cks'. If you have a bit of fun and heartily let fly in front of your children, bellowing a 'blow', 'blast', or 'oh, duck!', it will be habit-forming.

ABI1973

How to stop screaming at the kids

I think screaming at kids becomes a habit and one which I have found very difficult to break. Because you shout, they shout back, and before long, there is a screaming match. Try to catch yourself as you hear your voice getting louder, take a second, and bring it down a key. Very difficult initially but, with practice, it gets easier. Now I find myself saying to my son, 'I'm not shouting at you, please don't shout at me.' The pleasure I get from this is enormous.

ETS

Shouting at your children is as useful as stopping your car by honking the horn – everyone looks, but it has no effect. My child's primary teacher had more effect by lowering her voice than raising it.

HAPPYCANADIAN

How to discuss sex with your eleven-year-old daughter

Relax and chat about it as if it were anything else. Choose a time when you are both relaxed and comfortable. Answer all her questions. Try the whole bananas and condoms thing – she'll be really weird and embarrassed but she'll thank you for it one day. (Well, she may not thank you, but she'll accept it eventually.)

FABULOUSFEMINIST

How to encourage conversation at the dinner table

Sitting at the table with our four kids, my husband or I ask one of them, 'What was the best part of your day?' No matter how bad they feel their day has been, they have to try to think of something positive (even if it was only having their favourite sandwich for lunch). They then ask someone else the same question, until everyone has answered. This routine is then repeated, asking, 'What was the worst part of your day?' This has often led to interesting stories, revelations about things going on at school (like bullying), and as Mum and Dad also give their answers, the kids get to see that sometimes parents can have a bad day too.

SWEETHART

PARENTING – IT NEVER ENDS

or There's more to come. There's always more to come

How to get your teenage daughter to stop hating you

Wait however many minutes until she's over her fit.
Or, seriously, just be a good parent, and then wait until
she's an adult and realises what a good mother you were.
Most of us don't like our mothers until we are of an age
to appreciate what they've done for us (and that we've
essentially become our mothers).

STELLADORE

My mum used to tell me when I was a teenager, 'It's not
your parents you hate, but the power and control they
have over you.'

YANSIPAN

Hate is simply passion. She is saying she wants her own
way with all the determination of a single-minded,
hormone-fuelled adolescent. I used to say to my
daughter, 'I simply don't accept that being a teenager
means you are a special case. You need to behave in a
decent manner.' She seems to have turned out all right.

JOSA2

How to get your teenagers to communicate

Take them out for lunch, coffee or a walk, and just talk about anything before you ask what is up – if you keep things light they will open up. When they do, don't make a big deal out of anything they say, even if it does shock you there and then. Just shrug and go on to something else. Then go back to it a while later and they will open up more.

SAMMYC

How to communicate with your teenager

Try not to humiliate or shame them by listing their faults; it will make them feel judged which is one of the things they hate most. Remember, you can't judge and listen at the same time.

TWINK

Don't make light of their problems. Try to see things from their point of view so that it makes sense to you, rather than dismissing them with 'you're too young' or 'you'll get over it'.

SUUSE

How to give your precious fifteen-year-old daughter more freedom, and to accept her boyfriend when you don't want to let her go

Keep in mind that she won't learn any coping or problem-solving skills if you keep her wrapped in cotton wool. This is a really good time for her to learn them: while she's old enough to know what she's learning but still young enough to listen to you occasionally.

JILLAROO95

Give her her independence slowly so that you can both cope with the changes in your relationship. Accepting boyfriends is a tricky one, but you just have to do it, otherwise she will resent you. The first boyfriend probably won't last, and before you know it, they will have broken up and you'll have all the tears to mop up. She'll keep you occupied and busy for a long time to come!

EL

How to get your daughter away from a 'bad boy'

If he isn't doing drugs, or physically or mentally abusing her, then let it run its course with minimum comment from you. Open your home to them (I don't necessarily mean for overnights but just so she isn't skulking around outside the house). Kill him with kindness and that will take the heat out of the rebellion, if that is what the relationship is about. Keep a watching brief and don't comment unless you're asked. She knows how you feel, but keeping the door open for her is important.

ASHLING

How to decide what is the right age to allow your daughter to start shaving her legs

The decision to start shaving legs should be made by the girl in question. It really has nothing to do with her parents at all (unless she is a toddler!). As for hair growing back thicker and darker after shaving, this is complete nonsense. If a teen feels self-conscious about hair on her legs, surely it is more favourable for her to whip the lot off rather than have her obsess about something over which she has total control.

LADYDIGGER

How to help a grown-up child when his relationship breaks up

Let him know that he's strong enough to get through this. Don't be too pushy or invasive. Be there for him, without being overbearing, as this will, in most cases, simply cause irritation on your child's part. Also, never say anything along the lines of 'I told you this wouldn't work . . .' It might seem pretty obvious that one should avoid it, but some parents forget. Having your mistakes and faults pointed out to you after your heart has been stomped on does not make things any better.

DKARB

How to make a twenty-two-year-old son who still lives at home help around the house more and spend a little time as part of the family

Make a date to have a proper chat with your son and tell him how you feel. Find out his point of view and see if you can reach a compromise on the housework front. It will be hard, but you must try very hard not to get upset or angry. Try and set a family meal day, like Sunday lunch for example, at which you want to have the whole family eating around the table together. Open a bottle of wine and play at being 'The Waltons' for a couple of hours. This is a great time to catch up on news, gossip and so on. Failing that, put his rent up, hire a cleaner and go for a romantic dinner with your partner.

AMANDAF

How to cope with an empty nest

Keep in mind that your job as a mother was to raise your children so that they would become self-supporting. They have left the nest so you have succeeded and should give yourself some considerable pats on the back. Take a class, join a group, or volunteer for a cause.

JILLAROO95

SCHOOL

or A way of allowing young people to learn about the stuff we're too embarrassed to tell them, like smoking and drinking and sex

How to pick the right school for your child

Ask local parents which school their children attend and how they chose that school. Decide how far you are willing to travel to get your child to school. Then contact the schools you like the sound of and request a prospectus. Visit the school, with or without your child, depending on his or her age. You will soon get a 'feel' for the place: its environment, head teacher and playground, etc. Don't be afraid to ask questions! (Try not to be too influenced by the results – children's success and happiness at school shouldn't be measured purely on academic achievements.) Revisit with your partner or a friend whose advice you trust. Try not to be led too much by convenience or snobbery – trust your instincts!

EMILYJANE

How to help children feel more comfortable on their first day of school

Contact parents of children in the same class and arrange a play date before school starts so your child sees some familiar faces when they first enter the classroom. If the school will not give out that information you could ask them to extend the invitation on your behalf.

RUTH

Make sure they have a map of the school to look at and talk about. They can see where they have assembly, where they play and where they have lessons. It will make the whole school seem less intimidating and help them understand how the school works.

WEX

How to stop being bullied when telling teachers and parents hasn't helped

Keep a diary of exactly what the bully says/does and when, so you can back up what you're saying. It shows that this isn't something petty and you can feel more confident when you try to talk to someone. Send an email to your teacher. It might be that during the day they find it hard to concentrate, but if they are able to focus on your problem at a quieter time, then they have more reason to listen.

FABULOUSFEMINIST

If you've already told your teachers and nothing has happened, make a fuss – teachers should stand up for you over someone who is bullying you. Does your school have a support network? It might be worth going to see the school counsellor if there's one available to you. I was bullied at school and telling someone and continuing to tell someone works. Kick up a fuss until something is done to stop the bullying.

SEAGULL-PIE

If the nature of the bullying is physical, then try a self-defence class or something like boxercise. Try to go places with your friends or follow other people as this might put off your bully. And act confident and happy even if you're not. Visibly nervous people are much more likely to be bullied.

FABULOUSFEMINIST

How to save money and find a job (even though nobody's hiring) while at school

Saving money means making a budget and sticking to it. Start by recording all your expenses (even that pack of gum and fashion mag). After a week or so of recording expenses, see where you can make cuts. With respect to a job, think outside the box. Talk to the friends of your parents, aunts, uncles, grandparents, neighbours, etc., and see if they need ANYTHING, from babysitting to office filing to uploading their CD collection on to their iPods. Offer to teach the techie skills school children are famous for to 'older' people – how to use a digital camera, how to add numbers to a cell phone, how to work iTunes. You'd be surprised how many people could use such a lesson!

DEZG

How to study without getting stressed out

(1) Whenever you finish a topic, write revision notes about it. It'll make your life a lot easier when the exams come around. (2) If you don't understand something, DON'T put it off. Eventually you'll get swamped with stuff you don't understand. Ask your teacher to sit down and explain it outside class time. (3) There are a lot of university students who are looking to earn some cash through tutoring. They're cheaper, friendlier, and more flexible time-wise. (4) Don't be distracted by friends – try to get as much as possible done during school hours, so when you get home you can have some downtime. (5) Pick one night of the week where you are not allowed to do any work. It sounds a little odd, but if you know that you can't work on, say, Saturday night, then it'll prompt you to get work done earlier.

CATERIANNE

How to cram successfully if you have left revision too late

In general: quickly review the stuff you think you know pretty well, spend more time on the stuff you're more unsure of, and, if it really is too late, skip the stuff you never understood (if you didn't get it the first time, trying to learn it in the few precious moments before the exam is a real long shot). With any luck, you'll ace the stuff you know and do well enough on the stuff you revised, sufficient to compensate for the stuff you never understood.

DEZG

A good method is to try and condense a lot of information into a small phrase or word, where each initial stands for some information that is meaningful to the subject. Like the phrase 'Richard of York gave battle in vain' to remember the colours of the rainbow. I tried this recently with my exams and was amazed at how much information I could recall from just a seven-letter nonsense word I made up. If the word is funny, it's easier to remember.

PRINCESS87

How to deal with failure when you're struggling to complete university work because you know what you're writing is rubbish

Read more. If you're not writing well, it's because you don't know the topic well enough. Even if you're not a good writer, you can still write OK if you know your topic. Read first, then the writing is an exercise at the end of your course when you know the information well enough.

LEAHM74

How to raise money for school funds

We had some teachers who were up for a laugh, three of the male teachers agreed to have their legs waxed in front of an audience! It was great fun and we raised loads of money selling tickets to watch.

LILI2008

FAMILY

How to ask your parents to let you shave your legs

When my daughter was younger and couldn't figure out how to talk to me about something, she would email me. That way, she didn't have to look me in the eye, and she could take her time over her wording. By the same token, I could take the time to consider my answer. When my daughter emailed me asking if she could shave her legs, she listed her reasons very logically and in a mature manner, and I said yes!

ASILDEM

How to get your parents to give you more freedom

Always be up front about what's going on and you'll be surprised how much freedom you will have. Saying 'Mallory and Em are going to Westroads Mall after practice on Friday to look for a pair of jeans and asked me if I want to go. Emily's mom is driving. I'll be home no later than 9.30' will get a whole different reaction from 'Can I go to the mall with my friends?' Give your parents all the information they need and if plans change, call them so they can adjust their expectations.

WooHoo

How to not get involved in your husband's family fights

Divorce him. Otherwise, you're a part of his family and you're going to be involved. You can get out of the initial or immediate fray by removing yourself physically but the long-term situation is a concern of your husband's and, therefore, a concern of yours.

STELLADORE

How to deal with an interfering mother in-law

Can you direct her attention to something you don't care about, but which she does? Like, say, selecting the paint colour for the interior of the garage. If you can manage to get her to 'interfere' in ways that don't bother you (or bother you very little), then she'll have less time and energy for the things that really matter to you! One thing you really need to do is discuss the situation with your spouse and agree to a unified approach to what she does have a say in (like the dessert for Easter dinner) and what she has to keep her nose out of (like the number of, naming of or rearing of the kids) and how to deal with her when she crosses the line (you correct minor infractions in real time, he promptly addresses the big ones).

DEZG

How to get on with your mother-in-law

You'd be horrified if your partner was rude to your mother, so don't think you can get away with it, but there is also a limit. Be charming and polite, buy gifts, etc., but realise that many women don't get along with their mothers-in-law, so you're not alone. Do everything you can and never bitch about the situation to your partner. You can calmly explain that this went wrong because of . . . but don't bitch. That's what your friends are for.

FABULOUSFEMINIST

How to get your boyfriend's family to accept and like you

I like someone to help load the dishwasher, etc., without being asked – just get up and do it. What I do not like is someone who just sits there like a lemon and allows me to wait on her.

OPERATIX

How to get your adult son to accept your new partner when you're a widow

If your late husband had left you for someone else, your son would probably be furious with him and delighted that you'd met someone else to make you happy. However, speaking as someone who lost her beloved dad a couple of years ago, I have to admit that I'd struggle with anyone new in my mum's life. The best way you can approach this is to tell your son that you've been very lonely since his dad died and you don't want to be a burden to him or any siblings he may have.

LINDACEE

How to move back in with your parents after being independent

Remember, you are very blessed. You have people in your life who love you so much that they are willing to open their home to you and welcome you back. Not all parents would treat their adult children in this way. You are loved. Do your own laundry, cook for them regularly. Bring cheap, jolly flowers home from your shopping trips, and try not to slide back into the old way of doing things. You don't want to be treated as a child, so you must, on no account, behave like one. If they get a bit irritating at times, talk to them as though they were someone else's parents – it will help you stay firm and respectful and keep that teenage tone out of your voice. I'm thirty-eight and my mum can still bring out the sulky teenager in me!

ROSEBUDSMUMMY

How to deal with being estranged from your mother

Call her and tell her you want to have a relationship based on polite, gracious and courteous behaviour. Don't re-hash any of the problems you once had. This will make you the bigger person and the adult. Remember, she is your only mother, even if you think she is acting like a kid. Rise above it all.

HILLYMO

How to do Mother's Day on a budget

Take time to give your mum a break from her daily chores, clean the house, do the washing and make her some special meals, giving her time to relax and have the day off.

GABRIELLE

How to enjoy Mother's Day without your mum

If you know someone else who will be on her own, suggest getting together and having a day reminiscing about your mothers. This is a chance to enjoy the day and remember all the things your mum taught you.

HAYLEY

How to find a present for a new mum on Mother's Day

New mums crave sleep so the best present you can give her is a day off. Offer to look after the baby for a few hours, allowing her to relax and catch up on some much needed sleep.

SARAH

How to tell your mother that you don't like her boyfriend

Have a rational talk with your mother. Tell her that you don't like him and give her concrete reasons why this is so. Try your best to keep personal bias and emotion out of the conversation. If you sound calm and rational, you have a better chance of being listened to.

JILLAROO95

If you really feel it's important, do so, but be prepared for your mum to still see the man. She obviously likes something about him, and just because you've registered a complaint doesn't mean she will stop seeing him.

STELLADORE

How to tell your mother that you are homosexual

Be honest with your mum, but please be prepared for a number of different reactions. Whatever happens, your mum will always love you, but she may be scared for your future, she may be disappointed that it's less likely that you'll have kids, and she may be worried about her friends' reactions. All of those things are understandable to some degree and you may need to be patient with her.

LindaCee

How to deal with cantankerous parents

If they are like this most of the time, I think you may need to learn to just let their moods wash over you. Not in a rude way – just smile slightly, nod and don't let them get to you. You are your own person and entitled to your own opinions. Just don't force them on them and hopefully they will not do the same to you. I'm at the stage where I can see my parents have differing views on things, and some of the time I just have to count to ten, say nothing, and go with my own thoughts or ways of doing things. Once you do it a few times, it's like second nature!

MIMI18

How to sound upbeat when making telephone calls to an ill mother and carer father

The one thing that would mean more than anything is to let them know how much you love them. That's worth more than any amount of being upbeat. You could also tell them little amusing stories about things that happened to you that day. Let them into your life a bit and out of theirs, even for a few minutes.

Jillaroo95

This won't necessarily make you sound upbeat, but might be useful. Why not say you've been thinking about an episode in either their past or your mutual past and would like to be reminded of the details? It has to be a happy occasion. Then that gives them something nice to talk about to each other and to you.

CALI

How to take your elderly parents on holiday

For a start, try to remember that they're much slower at doing things than you, so try not to be irritated by that. Arrange things so that you and the children have about twice as much to do as they have, which will take the same length of time. Also, try to remember that much as they love you all, they probably rather enjoy being by themselves sometimes, too.

TROOPS

SENIORS

or What? I wish everyone would stop mumbling

How to age happily

NEVER act your age. Act your shoe size. At fifty-two I
am still climbing trees, playing football in the park, rock
pooling, building sand castles, and trespassing into fields
to pinch apples! And exercise.

LADYDIGGER

Taking care of yourself physically is important to aging
happily. Get regular check-ups, don't forget the dentist
or neglect your gums, exercise, moderation is the key in
dieting and sun exposure, but the most important thing
is don't neglect your spiritual side. Prayer, meditation
and acts of kindness to others help you enjoy life and
the wisdom of your years (especially if you volunteer at a
nursing or old people's home). And make sure you are on
top of your finances.

MASI

Flirt a little when you're talking to people; it always
raises a smile.

LUCYD

How to flatter your skin as you age

Use a light-reflecting foundation, soft colours on the lips, and light-coloured eye shadow (lilac is good). Also, if you have your hair coloured, have the front just a little lighter than the rest, it really brightens up the face.

BLONDIE5

How to improve your appearance

Concentrate at least three times a day on cultivating a pleasant, welcoming, cheerful expression.

TROOPS

How to look good in later years

Try, but not too hard. Remember, there's a fine line between sexy and slapper when over forty, so no bare midriffs off the beach, tattoos, or Goth eye make-up. If in doubt, ask your son or any other handy youth!

CORKYCHUM

How to improve your figure after sixty-five

Buy a new bra and have it fitted properly. We change. Accept it.

GAM

How to keep your mind sharp as you age

Take an Open University course, signing up for a degree in case you want to continue. It does wonders for morale, the mind, the memory (with magnesium, of course) and getting one up in the morning. I got my first degree at fifty-six and two more since. It is my all-time favourite pastime.

CANOPUS

How to be graceful in old age

Really concentrate on your posture – the older we get, the more inclined we are to be lazy and stoop. Above all, don't grunt and groan when you sit down and get up out of a chair.

LALA

How to do up a zip on the back of a dress or top if there's no one around to help you

Thread cotton or a long shoe lace through the zip and pull up.

JENNYWD

How to find a good dating website if you are sixty

Do you have any other single friends of your age? If so (male or female), you could make a pact to try out a few dating agencies and websites together. For the best websites, just spend a few hours on the internet and see which appeal to you. All sites will ask for your age and interests and help you hook up with similar people. No matter what your age, the only real answer is just to get out there and do it! The more you sign up to, the more people you will meet, and the more likely you are to meet someone you like. Just be very cautious at the beginning with anyone you meet (either virtually or in reality): don't trust anyone till they have earned your trust!

MICHELLE

How to find a suitable male in later life

You could always volunteer for a cause you feel strongly about. That would increase your chances of finding a man with at least some values similar to yours.

JILLAROO95

How to be everlastingly patient with a deaf companion

It is often said that deafness is the loneliest disability. I think this is particularly true if the deafness comes on through injury or aging and the deaf person has to struggle to pick up lip reading and sign language as an adult. My gran went very deaf and she was one of the smartest people I knew, really quick-witted. She got annoyed when people started to treat her as if she were stupid. Try to remember this when you communicate with your deaf friend.

MENOPAUSALMADAM

There are several members of my family who are deaf-ish and I find my best conversations take place on the telephone when they hold the earpiece close to their heads so they hear much better. This has really helped to build relationships as conversation is not so easy during big, noisy family parties.

JOSA2

Having been temporarily profoundly deaf due to an ear infection, my top tips would be these:

– always position yourself in full facial view of the person you are speaking to so he/she can read your expression and lips – this way they can take a stab at what you are saying. Turning away, even for a second, can blow your chances of communication!

– don't shout from another room or away from the person; they may hear your voice but not what you're saying, and that is frustrating. If you are approaching a deaf person, make some other noise, like banging on the floor, so that they're aware you are there.

HILARYGNORMAN

How to get over growing old alone

I'm old and I'm alone. I love it! I do what I want, when I want, have a great circle of friends, keep myself active and, by doing so, remain interesting. Don't concentrate on yourself. Look outward. If you hate your own company, everyone else will too.

BEACHY1

Instead of thinking about the years ahead of being alone, start thinking about all the things you want to do on your own before the new partner comes along. My dad has found love again recently at his local Evergreen club and he's eighty-three. He's no big Romeo but is just himself and does not pretend to be something he's not. If love can happen to him, it can happen to you too. Keep smiling at the world and saying yes to new opportunities – you never know what's just around the corner.

MANGOGIRL

How to cope with putting things in the wrong place

If it's things like keys and wallets, put a box or a basket on the hall table (or somewhere) and put everything in it when you get home. I also have a dish for my earrings and watch, etc., as I kept taking them off and leaving them lying around all over the place. Things get lost when they don't really have a home, so give them one and then you'll use it.

DISTRACTEDHOUSEWIFE

How to stay young in retirement

I am not retired, I am on permanent holiday. I wake up each morning and plan what to do that day. Life is wonderful.

REDLADY

How to avoid falls

Always sit on the edge of the bed to put on your knickers, tights, socks, trousers, whatever. Older people regularly fall over when getting dressed and undressed.

CALI

Never, ever have uncarpeted stairs or steps in your house. Coir matting is the absolute best, as it has substance and isn't slippery.

GAM

How to avoid slipping in the bath

Lay your damp flannel on the edge of the bath to give purchase when you get out.

TROOPS

How to ward off dowager's hump

To keep your shoulder muscles supple and strong and
ward off dowager's hump, do the following Pilates
exercise. Press your elbows into your waist and hold your
hands out in front of you as though holding a tray. Then
swivel your hands outwards, keeping your elbows tight
into your waist. Do six or seven back and forth, whenever
you think of it, at least four times a day.

CALI

How to get a job when you're over sixty and finding it very difficult

Take your date of birth off your CV. That at least might
get you an interview, and from there you can impress on
merit. It has worked for people I know.

PAULAMESSUM

WORK

or It's meant to be difficult, that's why it's called work

How to cope with bitching at work

Hear and see all, repeat nothing.

CAROLYN0001

This is so easy and it works every time. Be nice to them.
I mean so overwhelmingly nice that they have nowhere
to go with their bitchiness without looking like total
prats. Be a disgustingly saccharine-sweet little angel and
you will really confuse them!

RUNSFAR

How to get ahead at work when you're the only woman in the office

For a start, stop thinking that being female is a
disadvantage. In this day and age, office managers are
rarely the sexist pigs they were in the 1970s, and if you
show potential, they'll recognise and reward it. Just don't
back away from a challenge. If you don't like chairing
meetings or giving presentations, get yourself on a
course to overcome your fears. Let your manager know
that if he's looking for a second in command, you can be
relied on. In my experience, it's just down to putting the
hard work in, not what gender you are.

LINDACEE

How to make a stupid male colleague stop staring at you all the time

Just look him straight in the eye and ask, 'Are you all right?' If he says, 'Yes, why?', just say, 'You were staring at me and I wondered if there was something wrong.' That way you're putting the ball into his court and forcing him to excuse himself. The shiftier and more uncomfortable you are, the more encouraged he'll feel – you need to meet him head-on in a non-aggressive manner.

TizzysMum

How to stop your boss (or anyone) from making passes at you

Use unfriendly body language, 'blade' him with your body, i.e., turn so you are side on to him (if it is a him!). Don't stand with an open stance; this will make you look approachable.

DOZIGGY

How to get a co-worker to stop trying to pick you up

Have someone take a 'snugly' picture of yourself and a HOT male friend. Send yourself flowers, you know you deserve them anyway. Then, the next time buddy comes around, excitedly show him a picture of your new beau and the flowers he sent you.

MargaretMM

How to deal with a boss who is married but fancies you and wants to take you out on a date, and you don't want to

I've been in this situation and you've got to be completely up front with him. Say, 'You're married, and I don't do married men, so, no thanks.' Say it with a smile, and if you think his ego needs a bit of a massage, prefix your comment with, 'If you weren't married, things would possibly be different, but you are, so . . .' These days bosses can't get away with threatening your career if you don't play their game, so just be polite, but firm with him.

ELSIE

How to proof-read effectively and accurately

First, print it in hard copy. As you read through the hard copy, run your finger under each word slowly and say it aloud (feel free to close the door to your office/conference room/whatever!). When you hear text spoken slowly, you catch some of the things that your eyes or brain read into the draft when viewing on the computer screen.

DEZG

How to stay constantly motivated in a challenging new job

I find it hard to be motivated unless I'm working towards a specific goal. Find a worthwhile goal – like a promotion, special project, bonus, window office, maintaining employment for at least a year in this terrible economy, having all the VPs know your name within six months, whatever – and figure out the realistic steps to get there, and use that to motivate you. Where possible, add visual aids to your work space, from a photo of the islands you'd visit if you get that bonus, to a picture of the local skyline you'd see from that window office, or a magazine photo of a lady in a fancy business suit, anything to help you re-focus when you start drifting off.

DEZG

How to stop being a workaholic

There are two ways you can look at this: first is to look at the underlying reasons why you are a workaholic. Is your self-worth tied to your work? Is your home life bad? Do you feel indispensable? Once you've narrowed down the why, then do something about it. Get counselling or do something about the home situation, or realise that, realistically speaking, no one is truly indispensable. Or, secondly, if your workaholic tendency is a family trait that comes naturally to you, then the best way to deal with it is to wean yourself away from it in small steps, slowly, so that you can adjust. Perhaps start by not working so long at the weekend. Then stop working altogether at the weekend. Then go from there. That's what I did and I'm happy to say I'm no longer a workaholic.

JILLAROO95

How to avoid slouching over your desk and correct a terrible posture

My granddad was an upholsterer, and he always said that the key to avoiding slouching in a chair is by making sure the chair is the right height for you. Your legs should bend at ninety degrees, and if you're slouching over a desk, it means your desk isn't high enough: stick a telephone directory at each corner, and see if that makes a difference.

BEKKI007

How to feel less self-conscious when giving a presentation

Think of it as a mechanism to keep you on top of your game. People who are unself-conscious tend to be a bit too relaxed, when they should be making an effort, and it shows. By using your self-consciousness as a tool, it will become less of a burden to you and more of a benefit.

JILLAROO95

How to get a pay rise or promotion

Ask! Of course, do your research first. Know what is realistic in the market place and in your company. Be prepared with lists of your accomplishments, duties/tasks you perform that might be considered above your current position, accolades from clients, peers or superiors, or details of outside trade organisations or volunteer work you do which benefits the company, etc. Be flexible; if they can't give you a raise, what about stock options, a bonus or extra vacation? If they can't promote you, is there a lateral move that has more career advancement opportunities? If the answer is no, ask how you can improve or get to where you want to go (perhaps with management training or public speaking experience). Do it and then ask again. Note that timing is everything, so don't ask at the end of a profit-losing quarter or as the company is filing for bankruptcy.

DEzG

How to learn lines

These work for me.

(1) For long speeches, use a plain postcard and work your way down, covering your next line.

(2) For quick-fire dialogue, record the other person's lines on to an MP3 file (Audacity is a good program for this), transfer them to your iPod, and work through the scene while travelling.

(3) Once you know a scene quite well, barter with a neighbour to listen to you.

(4) For verse, dance as you recite it.

(5) For tough stuff with lots of metaphor and imagery, draw connected pictures in your head (or on your script).

(6) But, most importantly, however tired you are, always learn a scene the evening after rehearsing it.

Incidentally, if you find there's a particular bit you always forget, it might mean you haven't connected the character's thoughts behind the lines properly.

LEMMING

How to call in sick convincingly

I think the worst thing you can do is get someone to call in on your behalf. Most of us, even at death's door, can manage a brief phone call and I always get suspicious if a partner or friend contacts me. If you're going to take a sickie, keep the excuse simple and don't put on that fake 'I'm so sick' voice. Don't forget what was the matter with you when you return to work in case anyone asks if you're feeling better.

ZANNATHETRAINER

How to deal with a client who treats you like a servant, emailing 'orders', and who is difficult to build up a rapport with

This client may be a fast-paced, task-oriented person. That doesn't mean he's treating you like a servant; this is just the most efficient way of communicating. When it comes to business, not everyone is going to feel the need to be chummy and tell you to have a nice day or similar. Don't resent this person – instead, appreciate the fact that he's doing his best not to use up much of your time.

JILLAROO95

How to deal with a colleague who networks at social events in a very 'me me me' way, constantly looking over the shoulder of anyone she is talking to

If it's your shoulder they are looking over, why not ask a direct question, such as, 'Who exactly are you looking for?' It may be that this person is not fully aware they are doing it and you asking the question may focus their attention that bit more. If the behaviour annoys you that much, excuse yourself from their company and go and mingle with other people whose company annoys you less.

NUMPTIEHEID

How to survive if you're single, have been unemployed for nearly two years, living on benefits for too long and have run out of savings

First thing is get out of the house. Go for a walk every day – I know this might sound ridiculous but it's amazing how it will clear your head and give you more energy. Get into a routine! Keep yourself healthy and keep focused on what you ultimately want. Also, take a look at your belongings: anything you haven't used for two years, sell at a car boot sale or on eBay. This will keep you going until you land a job.

MIMI18

How to make your CV stand out

Have a look online for examples but just keep to relevant info, and don't go back through every job you had when you were sixteen. Keep the layout clear and precise and only to one page. Another good tip is to buy some heavy, good quality cream paper and envelopes. A nice cream, clean and unfolded sheet will show good presentation and stand out well among a large pile of white sheets.

JEMMALITTLEFAIR

How to dress for an interview

That really depends on the job! Try observing what people at your proposed new employment wear by visiting the work site when people are arriving for work or breaking for lunch. Use that as a guide, but make it a bit more formal for the interview. Avoid anything too sexy, too loud or which advertises too many brand logos. Don't wear flip-floppy mules or similar noisy shoes. Don't wear too much perfume or jewellery. Make sure everything fits well, standing and sitting. If it needs to be altered (tighter or more loose), get it done, otherwise you'll look sloppy.

DezG

How to relax at interviews

Be as prepared as possible. Research the company on the net or read the annual report. Make sure you know your way to the interview and be there ten minutes early. Get a good night's sleep and have a decent breakfast. Get your outfit ready the night before, down to shoes and accessories. Make sure shoes are polished and whatever you wear is clean, with hems and buttons fixed. Don't exaggerate your CV, practise the answers to questions like 'why should we hire you?' and 'what are your weaknesses?' – the type of questions that might throw you for six. Lastly, practise deep breathing to calm you, and you will be fine.

ASHLING

What really helped me is having a friend interview me before I went to the actual meeting. But make sure the friend is serious about it and offers some feedback. My friend actually asked harder questions than my interviewers!

STELLADORE

How to survive two months' work experience if you hate it and you do the worst tasks but it's compulsory

> For my work experience, I was asked to type phone numbers into a database, which should have taken a month but I got in early and stayed late (answering the phones when no one else was available, often to the boss, who thereby got to know my name). I finished the job fast, then made myself useful to people who were working on things that looked more interesting. By the end of the month, I had secured my first job and stayed with the company for thirteen years.

> ABI1973

How to cope with being made redundant

> Take a weekend off to re-group (yes, just one weekend). Next, think big-picture: this is about the global economy, not necessarily all about you or your performance. BUT it's a good opportunity to do some self-evaluation: were you happy at the job? Are there additional credentials that would make you more marketable? Were there areas of weakness that you could improve? Then, figure out next steps: do you need another job(s) now? Can you afford (time and money) to get additional education/training? Do you want to switch careers? Work out a game plan and schedule: CV, career counselling, head-hunters, job searches, networking, etc., and do that like it IS your full-time job (so, eight hours a day, five days a week).

> DEZG

TECHNOLOGY

*or As utterly dependent on others (to fix it when it
goes wrong) to a degree that you haven't been
since you were lying in an incubator*

How to extend the life of a phone battery

If you really want to increase your time between charges,
try de-selecting things you don't need. Bluetooth uses a
lot of power, as does Wi-Fi, so if you're not using those,
switch 'em off. GPS? Kills your battery, so don't use it if
you don't need to. The flash for the camera? Takes a fair
bit of power, so don't take photos in the dark.

MYFAVORITESOCK

How to conserve power when your computer's running out of battery

If you're working on a computer with a rapidly fading
battery (and you don't need the internet) turn off your
wireless access, it really chews up battery power.

TOOKE

How to conserve power and prolong your computer battery's life

Reduce the brightness to about forty per cent when
listening to music, avoid fully discharging the battery,
remember to put it on sleep mode when you're not using
it, and, most importantly, keep it cool, so out of the hot
sun, etc.

RUTH

How to keep your computer safe

Making sure you have anti-virus, anti-spyware and a firewall – and keeping them all up-to-date – will significantly reduce the number of problems you'll get. There are good, free programs for all of these; just use common sense, and remember prevention is better than cure.

NOVA7

How to promote your blog

In most forums, there is a signature box under your post so you can post the link to your blog there. Make it look nice, bold it, and centre it. Also, on Facebook or Myspace, there is always a space for your website.

PRISCILLAAA

How to keep your geek happy

Remember, geeks are people too, and here are some simple tips for keeping us happy.

(1) If we show you some gadget or computer/phone-based thing we think is cool, gasp in awe, even if it's the lamest thing you've ever seen.

(2) Remember, size IS everything. If we buy a fifty-inch LCD screen, it's because things genuinely look better the bigger they seem. Don't complain; just sit further back on the sofa, watch and enjoy.

(3) Never, ever mention Jar Jar Binks.

(4) Be aware that espresso is one of the major food groups and actually counts towards our five-a-day.

(5) If we buy one album by a band and like it, it is imperative that we then get every other album by that band. Absolutely imperative.

(6) Occasional sex would be quite nice but it's less important than an enormous TV.

MYFAVORITESOCK

How to speed up your computer

Start > Control Panel > Internet Options > Delete Temporary Files (includes cookies, pop up ads, etc. – picture shows cabinet being emptied of paper). If there is lots to delete, it will take a long time. Click OK when finished, then the red cross.

TOPTIPTWIN

How to know if a website is secure

It's always a worry when you enter credit card details online but there are ways to minimise the risk. Firstly, on pages where you enter financial details, the URL (long text string at the top) should change from 'http:// . . .' to 'https:// . . .' (secure mode). In addition to this, a padlock icon should appear in the bottom of the browser window. In the UK particularly, the site may subscribe to the 'Verified by Visa' and 'MasterCard Secure' programs. To join these, your data needs to be managed according to stringent rules and there are large penalties should they fail to do this. If you're still unsure, check to see if they have a reasonable customer care set-up (call their number and ask them what they do with credit card details following a purchase) or do a Google search on 'company name + complaints'. If other people have had big problems, don't use the site!

MYFAVORITESOCK

How to fix sticky keys on a recently tea-soaked keyboard

Make sure your keyboard is unplugged/switched off, grab an old toothbrush, wrap a baby wipe round the bristles, and gently rub. You can do the same using a cocktail stick to get into the awkward bits.

FUNNYGIRLSHELL

How to prevent losing your camera

Take a photo of your contact details at the beginning of every memory card, so if you lose your camera, the finder will know how to find you to give it back.

RUTH

How to remember passwords

There are lots of services that require you to change your password periodically and some don't allow you to use your previous ten passwords. It is a safety measure but can be annoying. You can cheat the system by using the same word and just increasing its accompanying number, e.g. 'password1', 'password2', and then go back to back to 'password1'. You could correspond the current month with the number as well, whatever works for your memory. But never write it down.

NAVSTIPS

I work in a call centre and most people use their kids' names, but my favourite password was . . . 'iveforgotten'! Genius.

JAYNEYM

How to make sure your children are safe online

The bottom line is that, as long as you know less about your computer and the internet than your eight-year-old does, you can't control or monitor what he/she does online. Ultimately, if you want to keep them safe, get to grips with the technology. The best way to know what your kids are doing is to be there when they use the computer and then be very honest and up front with them should they stumble upon something untoward (and they will). As they get older, you will have less and less control over what they can and cannot look at, so the best thing you can do is equip them now to deal with the dodgy stuff on the internet in an open and honest way when they find it!

DAVLINDS

Keep their computer in a public place, such as the family room or kitchen with the screen facing the room.

TOOKE

Why you should turn your computer off

Apart from wasting energy, it can ruin the bearings in your hard drive. So turn your computer off every night to extend its life span.

RUTH

TRAVEL

How to barter/haggle as a woman in Eastern markets

I did this in Turkey every time I bought something and it worked every time! Ask the price of something without your boyfriend or male friend or husband around (if you're on your own, this works too). See what price they give you, then say politely, 'I think I will have to check with my husband.' Go around a corner out of sight and take a note out of your purse of what you are actually willing to pay, head back and tell them your husband would only give you X amount to spend. Every time, they respected the decision of 'the husband' and would take the amount I offered. Easy negotiating, with no hassle whatsoever!

NELLYPRDIRECTOR

How to avoid unwanted advances from men while travelling

Move with purpose and as if you know where you're going, even if you don't. Often, men will approach women who look unsure, since this can be perceived as a sign of weakness, and predatory types tend to take advantage of that. They are less apt to approach a competent-looking woman. There are also men who like a challenge, so if they still approach you, I suggest giving them a blank, unwavering stare until they go away.

JILLAROO95

How to build the perfect sand castle with your children

Damp sand (not wet) makes the best sand castles. Have your children direct how it will be made and put yourself in the position of their 'helper'. Bring shells and stones and let them decorate the castle. Ask them to tell you the story behind this particular castle.

JILLAROO95

How to do something useful when you're travelling

Check out www.StuffYourRucksack.com to see if you can take something that's needed wherever you're going. It might be pencils for a school or a football for an orphanage – places and requests are listed. This is a brilliant idea that really deserves support.

CALI

Check out the local culture and see if you would like to learn something from them. Cooking courses are popular where you learn the local cuisine (this is popular in Thailand). Learning a new skill is always very fulfilling. If you are travelling to a Third World country, do some research into programmes which help the less fortunate and see what they are asking for.

BEULAH

How to dress comfortably on safari

When travelling in Africa, wear a support bra for the safari. VERY bumpy roads. GREAT adventure!

SHEILA

How to find great local restaurants when travelling

Often, when you ask your hotel's concierge or doorman for suggestions of a restaurant, you'll get the name of whichever restaurant has given the biggest back-hander. So try asking the porter or someone lower down the 'food chain' in the hotel's staff. They are less likely to have been bribed.

MONICA

How to keep young children amused on long car trips

Play 'spot the car' of a certain make or colour. Every time you spot one, you have to shout out whatever your chosen make or colour of car before anyone else does.

BOOBOO

How to travel with a baby and arrive looking unscathed

Accept that you are going to end up wearing whatever you've fed your child and that you won't be able to change – so wear black and carry a fresh, bright scarf to wear on arrival.

HAPPYCANADIAN

How to travel on long-haul flights with small children

Having travelled ten-hour flights with children every year since they were born, I've learned to go to a novelty store a week or so before the flight and buy small, inexpensive games or toys. They'll preoccupy children for a short while, and it doesn't matter if they get lost. But here is the real edge: wrap them individually and number them, making up a set for each child. Let the kids see them, and tell them that they can't open no. 1 until we are at the boarding gate, no. 2 after our meal is cleared away, etc. For my kids, it was a perfect distraction and reward – right up to the last one on arrival. (Don't forget to leave one end of each package open so that it can be inspected by customs if necessary.)

HAPPYCANADIAN

How to drive on the correct side of the road in a foreign country

Get a brightly-coloured sticker with an arrow on it pointing in the direction of the correct lane. Stick it on the steering wheel. This way, you see it as soon as you get in the car and can keep on checking.

PANDSY

How to drive safely in snow and ice

Keep an old piece of carpet at least 1 x 3 feet in your car to put under a skidding tyre. It's more effective than salt or grit which can just disappear into the snow.

CALI

Being in a higher gear does help and you can even do it in most automatic cars. Check whether there's a gear lock button to lock you into second or third.

TROOPS

How to find which side your petrol tank is on when pulling up at the petrol pump

If you look at your fuel gauge display (on the dashboard), you'll see a little petrol pump icon: the handle (there may also be an arrow) on the pump indicates which side the petrol tank is. So, if the handle on the pump (or the arrow) points to the right, your tank will be on the right and therefore the driver's side of your car. If it's on the left, then the tank is on the left or the passenger's side.

JULIEG

How to freshen the smell of your car

A few drops of your favourite essential oil on dampened cotton wool is a good idea. You will have to refresh it every few days but it's a pleasant and natural way to freshen your car.

ASHLING

Buy a bar of soap in a scent that pleases you and just leave it in a paper bag in the car. It emits a clean, light smell.

DEZG

How to stop children from fighting in the car

If the kids are knocking seven bells out of each other in the car and refuse to be quiet, turn on Bach's Toccata and Fugue in D minor at full volume. It renders them speechless and teaches them something at the same time.

COUGAR

How to park a car

Parallel parking can be tricky, but if you are parking in front of shop windows, use your reflection in the glass to help you. Often, we stop well short of the room available, but if you look at your image in the glass, you can see how close you are – if your reflection isn't touching, then neither are you.

SHEENAMF

How to save money on petrol

Slow down. If you drive at 70 mph, you use 9 per cent more petrol than if you drive at 60 mph. And if you drive at 80 mph, you use an unbelievable 25 per cent more petrol than if you stick to 70 mph.

BooBoo

How to write the perfect letter of complaint about a disastrous holiday

Never give up, and be prepared to write at least three letters. Companies know that most people can't be bothered to write a lot of letters and use this to their advantage. From my experience, when making a complaint about anything, a company's first response is to fob you off by offering no compensation, in the hope you'll get bored and go away! In the second letter, they generally offer some company vouchers, which doesn't cost them anything (and often means you end up spending more money with them!). If your complaint's not serious, then you could accept the vouchers, but if it is serious, then don't accept them. Complain again and, nine times out of ten, you will be successful by the third letter. Also, contact trading standards/CAB, etc., and advise the company of this in your complaint letter.

LOULI

How to cope with a fear of flying

It probably sounds unlikely, but a friend of mine does this and she says it helps to pretend you're on a bus. Close your eyes and imagine yourself on a coach travelling on the motorway. After a while, the occasional patch of turbulence will feel no different to a bumpy road or pothole.

FAWN

How to get upgraded on a flight

This is a trick I once used and it actually worked.
On the way to the airport, buy a box of chocolates.
When checking in, say, 'Last time I was here, one of
your colleagues upgraded me. It's the best thing that
has ever happened to me and I promised to bring her
a box of chocolates next time I was passing through.
Unfortunately, I can't remember her name, so could you
put this in your rest area so you can all enjoy them?'
Then do not ask for an upgrade, just smile and look
around nonchalantly. In my case, the check-in lady was
so shocked and thrilled, she immediately upgraded me!
Warning: this does take some nerve. And, if it doesn't
work, all you've lost is a box of chocolates.

AMBER

How to stop your ears from hurting when landing in an aeroplane

When learning to SCUBA dive, you have to equalise
your ears as you dive deeper – the same technique
works in aeroplanes and high-rise elevators! In SCUBA,
you're taught to:
(1) take a deep breath,
(2) close your mouth and squeeze your nose shut, and
(3) slowly, gently try to exhale.
As your mouth and nose are shut, it forces the air to
your ears, and works to equalise them.

DEZG

How to carry toiletries and pamper yourself during a flight

When purchasing your cosmetics, ask the salesperson if there are any samples '. . . because I have an upcoming trip.' Since you've just made a purchase, they are MUCH more likely to share samples (and more of them) than they'd be for a random sample-blagger. Plus, as these are products you're already using, your airline pampering won't result in adverse reactions! Don't wait until just before landing to start your pampering – everyone else will be trying to freshen up and you won't be relaxed while people are banging on the restroom door!

DEZG

How to avoid tummy upsets when travelling

Wherever you are travelling, try to eat the local yogurt. This has local bacteria and can help you avoid a tummy upset.

ROSEPINK

How to stop travel sickness

Put your middle finger and index finger on your wrist (as if you were taking your pulse). Put pressure on it, and it should ease the sick feeling.

FLOURESCENTADOLESCENT

How to get cheaper rail fares

In many cases, if you are travelling with two or more friends, buy all the tickets together, then split the cost. It works out cheaper than buying them individually as you get a group discount. A very friendly ticket attendant once gave me and my friends this tip.

OHKNICKERS

How to pack a straw hat in hold luggage so that it doesn't come out a crushed mess at the other end

Stuff the hat with socks or underwear and then carefully pack other clothes around it. That way, it doesn't get squashed. Obviously, don't pack it right next to or under heavy things like shoes or books.

ANITA123

How to pack shoes

The little plastic shower caps that you get in hotels are great for packing shoes in. This makes sure that the rest of your clothes, as well as your shoes, are kept separate and protected. Place socks, knickers, etc., inside your shoes.

DEBORAH

How to prevent bottles from leaking while travelling

Before you pack your plastic bottles for a plane trip, gently squeeze some of the air out of the bottle, and then tightly close. No more leaking bottles when you arrive at your destination.

BOBBIE

How to travel long-term with absolute minimal clothing

When backpacking for a year, I learned to take only black underwear, so it could double as a bathing suit wherever I ended up swimming. In Egypt, black panties and a black T-shirt worked in the Nile.

HAPPYCANADIAN

How to deal with loss of money, passports, etc.

Before you travel, send yourself an email containing the following: a scan of your passport, your credit card issuer's contact telephone number, serial numbers of travellers cheques, airline ticket numbers and contact details of airline, contact details of next of kin, and any other information which may be lost while travelling. If you have a problem, you can usually access your emails and get the info you need to put things right.

ROSEPINK

SAFETY

*or Luckily, the heart-stopping and unmistakable
sound of an axe-wielding maniac stumbling around
your kitchen in the middle of the night will almost
always be a figment of your imagination*

How to keep safe

Be proactive. If you are walking alone, always know
where your mobile phone is and where your keys are,
so you are prepared. Be confident and walk briskly.
Predators tend to prey on easy targets, and if you are
walking fast and seem strong, you are less of a target.

Melie

When you're out and about, always be aware of who's
around you on the street. Don't walk with your head
down, texting on your mobile with your handbag
dangling off one arm. A man tried to mug me once
when I was taking money out of a cash machine (in
broad daylight on a busy street!). He put his arm around
my neck and I reacted by launching myself backwards,
turning around, pushing him away from me, and roaring
straight into his face like a lion. (Thank you, Oprah!) It
scared the heebie-jeebies out of him.

GUINEAPIG

How to guard your handbag in public

Best of all is to use a bag with a zip (so that you can close it entirely) and a long strap that you can sling diagonally across your body, so nothing can be removed surreptitiously. If it has a shorter handle or strap, when you are sitting down (in a restaurant or loo), you can leave your handbag on the floor between both feet with the handle/strap around your ankle (or around the leg of your chair). Just be sure to unhook it and pick it up before you stand up!

ABII973

How to be safe when meeting someone you have met on the internet, to either buy from, sell to, or date

Meet in a public place, tell someone where you are going, and if they haven't heard from you by a certain time, to call you. Or go with someone to meet this person. Make sure you stay on neutral ground and, if you feel uncomfortable, LEAVE!

HARRIET I

Don't tell them where you live or arrange for them to come to your house for the pick-up. Don't give them your phone number, take theirs.

GUINEAPIG

How to deter burglars

Experiment with lights to leave on while you are out. Go and stand in the street and look critically at your house. Does it look as though someone is home? Choose which curtains to leave mostly drawn and lamps on so that it looks as though you are in, but upstairs.

ROSEBUDSMUMMY

If your garden is close to a downstairs window, plant prickly shrubs. You can get pretty, flowering ones with spiky stems and leaves. That will help. Or plant window boxes; they will get in the way of potential intruders and draw attention to them trying to break in. They will find an easier home to try.

ASHLING

How to secure your house while you're away

Make sure you cancel any deliveries, such as newspapers or milk, as these can pile up and advertise an empty house. Double check your locks and make sure your house insurance is up-to-date and that any new or expensive items are included in your policy. Get some timers for your lights and sockets, and set a radio or television to come on at random intervals. Ask a friend to check on your home while you're away and leave them contact numbers for any emergency.

NOREEN

How to avoid being car-jacked

Be aware of the following car-jacking ploy. You unlock your car and get inside. Then you lock all your doors, start the engine and shift into reverse. You look into the rear-view mirror to back out of your parking space and notice a piece of paper stuck to the middle of the rear window. So you shift back into park or neutral, unlock your doors and jump out of your car to remove that paper or whatever it is that is obstructing your view. When you reach the back of your car, the car-jackers appear out of nowhere, jump in and take off.

BOOBOO

How to be safe in a car park

Women have a tendency to get into their cars and just sit there (getting organised, making a list, etc.). Don't do this! A rapist or car-jacker could be watching you and this is the perfect opportunity for him to get in on the passenger side. As soon as you get into your car, lock the doors and drive away.

TOOKE

How to cope when you are being mugged

If a robber demands your handbag, do not hand it to him. Toss it away from you. He is probably more interested in your handbag than in you and he will go for the handbag. Run like mad in the other direction.

PINGLE

How to defend yourself

The little finger is weak, so if anyone grabs hold of you, go for his little finger, and pull like hell, the rest of the hand has to follow. Act quickly, though, before he has time to think about what you're doing. Eyes make a good target too, so stick your fingers in. And give the top lip a good hard twist. The solar plexus (stomach) is also a good place to hit if you're being attacked; that'll wind him. A hard shoe sole run down a shin will hurt too, as will a poke from a couple of fingers into the base of the throat. Don't worry about hurting a would-be attacker – self-preservation is your first concern.

COLIYTYHE

How to keep safe when staying in hostels or cheap hotels

Buy a large door wedge to take with you and use it every night. This is also good for those sharing houses who don't want unwelcome advances in the night.

PATSHARP

How to make sure your child is as safe as possible on his/her gap year

If he is trustworthy, give him a credit card to be used in emergencies only. Incentivise him not to use it frivolously by saying you'll give him a certain amount of money when he gets home if it's unused.

GIA

Agree that she will call or email you, just to check in, every forty-eight hours or so. Ask her to give you a copy of her itinerary and to let you know if she decides to make any changes. Although she is no doubt longing to spread her wings, she's probably a bit scared too.

ORINDA

How to sleep soundly when travelling alone

Always check the evacuation routes as soon as you get to the room, so you won't panic if there is an emergency. Check the route and count alcoves/doors so you can find your way in the dark. For security, if there isn't a chair to jam under the door handle, use items in the room to 'booby trap' the area by a door or window, such as plastic cups, crisps from the minibar, or anything loud or breakable.

VILLANOVA

How to call the emergency number anywhere

Wherever you are, you can call the international emergency number on 112. It will use any nearby signal and even works when the keypad is locked.

RUTH

GIFTS

or I love it! (How could you?)

How to buy presents for a geek/nerd

Generally, there is one rule to remember: worthwhile technology costs money. If it's a cheap gadget, it's probably not worth having. Good-quality tech gadgetry costs in the hundreds of pounds – think Sony eBook or Amazon Kindle 2 rather than a USB Christmas tree. If that's out of your price range (and it probably is), just fall back on the trusted geek staple of humorous and/or ironic T-shirts. A good website to visit is thinkgeek.com. Another is theonion.com. Also, anything with even an oblique reference to R2-D2 on it is automatically cool. Happy Birthday/Christmas to us . . .

MYFAVORITESOCK

If you're completely stuck on ideas, ask for a gift list – what geek doesn't enjoy compiling lists?

SIUCRA

How to find the right present for my eighty-five-year-old grandmother

Photocopy her wedding photo, birth certificate, picture of her house, grandchildren, pets, favourite flowers, or even photograph her engagement ring, etc. Cut them out and then decoupage them on to a tray. Use lots of coats of varnish to make a tough surface. She'll use it every day and see all her nice memories on it.

PATSHARP

How to hide presents from your children

If you have grandparents living nearby, hide them at their house. It's foolproof.

ASHLING

How to know whether to bake your guy a cake on his twenty-first

The first year I was with my boyfriend (now husband), I did a 'bloke' cake. I bought a chocolate sponge base and iced it with the words 'ARSE' in beautiful blue icing and surrounded with a ring of Smarties. He nearly wet his pants laughing and still tells his friends about it five years on. On another note, there is much truth to the saying 'the way to a man's heart is through his stomach'. Wise words!

PUSSYCATLOVER

I made my husband a two-tier pork pie instead of a birthday cake a couple of years back. Men often prefer savoury food to sweet things and are easily amused by things out of scale.

DISTRACTEDHOUSEWIFE

What to buy your boyfriend for Christmas

Don't ask him what he wants. He doesn't want what he wants. What he REALLY wants is to be delighted and surprised by your choice. Any woman who can get a man a favourite shirt always goes on a pedestal. A day out – driving steam trains, rock climbing, discovering falconry – may be expensive, but you could share it. The autograph of his favourite sports star, made out to him. A really nice shaving brush. A poker lesson. Fifty feet of rope. An acre of rainforest. A voucher for some of your time to do with you as he wishes. Not socks.

LEMMING

What to buy a pregnant friend

A pregnancy massage, or a simple manicure/pedicure and the offer to babysit while she takes it (if she has other children). It's a treat that's all about her at a time when most people will be talking to her about babies.

ABI1973

How to get the gifts you want on Valentine's Day, not what he wants you to wear

My husband is on the autistic spectrum, so he doesn't really 'get' hints – I have to tell him directly what I want, and remind him frequently of important dates. Once you get over the socially accepted idea that he should somehow just know these things, it is so much easier. I tell him what I want, and don't end up with rubbish. He knows what to get and doesn't panic. Everyone's happy, and we have a great day with no rows or disappointment. It's just a case of getting past the ridiculous idea that our partners are only romantic if they can mind-read!

ANGIEGW

How to give the perfect wedding gift

If you know their honeymoon plans and interests, consider treating the couple to something indulgent during their honeymoon, like a couple's massage, a hot air balloon ride, a dinner at a posh restaurant, a day of SCUBA diving, tickets to a theatre performance, etc. Have an announcement of the gift (or a gift certificate) sent to their hotel suite. Helping to create wonderful memories can be more meaningful than a vase or a set of towels (no matter how useful).

DEzG

How to wrap presents for young children

Buy big sheets of paper and get the children to decorate them.

BooBoo

How to write a perfect thank you note

Always send it sooner rather than later. If it's thanking someone for a present, always give some specific detail about how/why you love it and how it's being used.

COLIYTYHE

CHRISTMAS

or Brace yourself . . .

How to buy Christmas presents on a budget

Send a newsletter to the adults on your present list and tell them that present-buying is getting out of hand. Most people will find the proposal a great relief.

JENNYWD

You could make sweets and cookies and wrap them in coloured cellophane. If you can crochet or knit, make some scarves. Or bottle some home-made chutney. Another good idea is to buy fabric remnants and sew travel make-up bags for the women and toiletry bags for the men.

JILLAROO95

One Christmas when I had no money, I gave my family vouchers for my time. To my brother, I gave a voucher for me to wash his car, and to my father, I gave cooking a three-course dinner. I made the vouchers up on nice cards.

PUSSYCATLOVER

How to stop yourself going broke at Christmas

Hit the January sales. You can pick up loads of Christmas stuff at a fraction of the price in January. I try to buy all of my wrapping paper, cards and decorations, and then store them away until December.

SOPHIE08

How to tell my friends I don't have money to spend on them this Christmas

I buy all my presents at charity shops and buy really outlandish things for my friends. Nothing over five pounds is permitted. My list last year included a jigsaw of the M5 motorway. My friends love them and remember exactly what I buy them each year (probably with horror).

LADYDIGGER

How to not gain weight over Christmas

Small helpings! I put everything on my plate, just in tiny, tiny amounts.

LYNZBEAR21

How to make brandy butter look more appealing

Some icing sugar sifted through a sieve sprinkled on top.

OPERATIX

How to make cranberry sauce for turkey

One part sugar, one part water, four parts cranberries. Cook until the cranberries start splitting.

JILLAROO95

How to make your house smell like a Christmas tree

I'm an essential oils fan and at Christmas use frankincense or pine and cinnamon oil in an oil burner for a lovely festive smell.

ASHLING

How to survive Christmas Day

Prepare in advance. Peel vegetables the night before. Make use of ready-prepared foods. Don't try anything new. Follow a rough timetable. Wash up as you go along. Bribe the children and husband to lend a hand. Try self-hypnosis and go on to automatic pilot mode. Pretend you're sexy Nigella. Dress up but wear comfortable shoes. Record programmes you're desperate to watch and don't argue when others want to watch something different. SMILE. Whatever happens, pretend it doesn't matter, you meant it to happen!

EIRLYS

How to survive Christmas

From 1 December, try to do/organise/plan one thing each day, however small or large. It could be as simple as deciding which crackers you want or as (potentially) complex as working out your cooking timetable. It may help spread the load and allow you to feel more in control.

LABINK

Start creating your own Christmas traditions, based on things that make you happy.

JILLAROO95

How to arrange lights perfectly on a tree

Plug them in and turn them on first to make sure they're still working. Then put them on the tree before you put on any other decorations.

ANITAL

How to prevent cats pulling decorations off your Christmas tree

Have a spray bottle filled with water nearby at all times and spritz them with water when they start being cheeky.

FABULOUSFEMINIST

ECO

How to help the environment and make your daily commute a little less dull

Help the environment by starting a car pool. This may make your commute that little bit less stressful by providing you with time to catch up with a friend or save you time by discussing work issues before you get to the office.

BooBoo

How to dispose of an old bicycle and make a difference

Try contacting your local homeless shelter and see if they would like to give your old bicycle to one of the homeless people they help. If it's beyond use, donate it to bikeworks.org.uk and they will recycle it for you.

AALIYAH

How to dispose of old glasses and make a difference

Donate your old glasses to a developing country and bring sight to the visually impaired. In some African countries the price of a pair of glasses can exceed three months' wages. Donate to Vision Aid Overseas, the Second Sight Project or hand them into any branch of Vision Express.

TOOKE

How to cut down on your energy bill

By adding draught excluders to windows and doors you can save money on your energy bill. These are cheap items to buy or make, and earn their cost back very quickly.

XTHATSCUTEX

How to reduce heat loss from your radiators

If you can't afford expensive radiator-back insulation panels you can make your own: flatten a cardboard box cut to the size of the radiator, cut slits in it so it slides over the brackets easily, cover it in tinfoil and tape down. This can cut your heating bills by about fifteen per cent!

JADSIA

How to reduce waste paper

You can reuse most as scrap paper. Sheets can be cut down to smaller sizes and stapled together – ideal for leaving by the phone to scribble down messages.

LUCYD

We waste loads of paper just by having huge margins so pull them across and up and down. I'm sure this could save a forest.

FABULOUSFEMINIST

How to recycle magazines

Drop them off at the local hospital waiting area.

SANDRASIMMONS

How to recycle junk mail

Keep the envelopes most junk mail comes in for school use – dinner money, trip money, swimming money, letters, etc.

LJH

How to reduce junk mail

Unwanted mail can be curtailed by writing 'refused – return to sender' on the envelope. Post it, and after a bit they will take your name off their database.

CANOPUS

How to recycle in the home easily

Join freecycle.org. You won't believe the things they take: from a few bricks to door handles, paper, etc.

JADSIA

How to recycle and update your wardrobe

Arrange a clothes swap evening. Replace items you no longer wear and enjoy a fun night in with friends.

TOOKE

How to reuse water from a condensing dryer

Simply pour it into a bottle and use it in your steam iron. It's even better if you use fabric conditioner as it retains some of the fragrance.

KALW

How to save the environment

I find that by booking my grocery shopping online, I only buy what I really need, as I don't get to see the bargains or other temptations which I would spot in the aisles of an actual shop. This means that I waste a lot less food – I now throw away virtually nothing. Also, learn how to store your vegetables properly, such as putting potatoes, onions and bananas in bags designed to prolong their lives, so again you are likely to throw away less. And get used to making things out of leftovers and saggy veg. I use Ocado's low-emission green vans, which make multiple deliveries in one journey, rather than driving to the shop myself.

ABI1973

PETS

or The sane ones in the house (usually)

How to get a bird back into his cage

Draw the curtains and turn out the lights. Birds don't like to fly in the dark. You can then pick it up gently and put it back in the cage.

PATSHARP

How to catch a mother hen and her chicks free-ranging in your garden

You are better off trying to catch them either late in the afternoon or early in the morning. They are a lot more settled at this time. Stand back so as not to spook them and then throw a towel over them. When you pick them up they will flap; be firm but gentle and hold their legs together.

FELICITYCP

How to get rid of cat smells in the house

If you've got a cat that has weed or sprayed somewhere, clean the area with warm water that has had non-biological washing powder/liquid added to it. When the area has dried, use Olbas Oil or vinegar to discourage the cat from using the area again. Always have one litter tray per cat, plus a spare. Cats are very fussy about sharing their 'toilet' arrangements.

MISSGALORE

How to get a young cat to stop using a litter tray and start going outside for the toilet

Sprinkle cat litter outside. He'll soon get the idea.

LUSHLADY

How to stop the local feral cat using the cat flap and eating all the food in front of your very timid cat

A couple of years ago, I had the problem of a feral tom breaking in and fighting my own cats. What I did was trap the feral and take him to the local cat rescue centre. I then paid for him to be neutered. This was much cheaper than all the trips I was making to the vet with my own cats! There was a happy ending in that after a while he was eventually re-homed.

MENOPAUSALMADAM

How to stop your cat scratching the wallpaper

Get an empty, well-cleaned squirty bottle (like the ones the bathroom cleaner or window cleaner come in) and fill with water. Whenever the cat scratches, immediately squirt it with water. It won't harm the cat but it will shock it enough to make it stop. If you do that every time, your cat should eventually leave the wallpaper alone.

TANYA123

If there is one area of the wall your cat always scratches, hang tinfoil there for a few days. Cats hate the sound and feel of tinfoil and they will not touch it or go anywhere near it. After a few days, the cat will not go near the wall or area that he normally scratches and you can remove it.

LIBBYHEWS

How to successfully introduce a new kitten into the home if you already have a dog

Put the cat in one of those wicker cat baskets (the ones with the wire door) and then take the dog (on a lead with someone it trusts holding it) into the room where the cat is. Do it in small stages, letting the dog sniff around the basket, and eventually let the cat out (with the dog still on the lead) to see how the dog reacts.

FLOURESCENTADOLESCENT

How to get pet hairs off your furniture

Use a washing up glove to remove pet hairs off any fabric. Rub over in one direction and hair will lift and clump together.

KTIGERLILLY

How to prepare a pet's travel crate

Put a worn item of clothing that belongs to you in your pet's basket while travelling; your smell will soothe it.

CLIO

How to stop a dog pulling on the lead when food, muzzles and harnesses don't stop him

Take your dog somewhere safe, and when he starts to pull, drop the lead and turn and walk the other way. Alternatively, you can use a long training leash if you don't want to drop the lead. Call him back to you and give him a treat when he comes. Keep repeating. He'll get the message that pulling on the lead is going to get him nowhere.

ALI161

How to cure a dog's bad breath

You can buy charcoal biscuits in pet shops, little bone-shaped ones. My dogs loved them and they help with bad breath.

VALENTINE

How to brush a dog who hates it

In one hand I hold his favourite treat and hold it just so he can have tiny nibbles. He's so preoccupied with getting the treat, he barely notices I'm brushing him. Normally, he would bite the brush or I would have an endless chasing frenzy.

PANDSY

How to get rid of the smell of fox poo when your dog has rolled in it

My two Labradors love to roll in fox poo. I find cleaning it out with your dog's own shampoo still leaves the smell behind. Bicarbonate of soda is the answer: once he's washed and dry, just sprinkle some into your dog's coat and brush out.

THEDOGSDAD

How to get your dog to accept a new dog

The best way to introduce new dogs is in a neutral area, not at home. Have a dog gate so they can sniff each other, but without the risk of a fight. You need to get your old dog to associate the new dog with good things, so give him treats when he is around and lots of fuss. The most important thing is to give them time and be patient; it may take weeks or months.

FELICITYCP

How to give your dog a shiny coat

Give him a little oil in his food every day. It can be
vegetable or olive oil, whatever you have handy.

JENNYNIB

How to house train your dog without spending money

This takes loads of time, not loads of money. The advice
given to me when I got a puppy was to take her out
at regular intervals – so every two to three hours, and
always immediately after she eats, drinks a lot, or wakes
up. You don't need money, just consistency.

STELLADORE

How to relieve a dog that's bitten or licked a toad

Give it a bowl of tomato juice.

CALI

How to stop a dog fight

Tread hard on one of the feet of the dog whose jaws
are locked on the other. Their yelp of pain will free the
locked jaws.

CTUSSAUD

My vet told me to get a stick and push it into the
attacking dog's bottom!

PATSHARP

Cold water from a distance is definitely the best idea – it
makes them jump enough to separate and you don't have
to get too close. Turning a hose on them (if there's one
handy) usually works best.

SEAGULL-PIE

How to stop dogs chewing on unwanted things

Purchase a bottle of oil of cloves (used for toothaches). With a paper towel rub it on the item or area the dog has taken to chewing. Be careful because the oil is hot to the touch (although you can wash it off with soap and water). The dog can't take the intense smell and will be put off chewing. It needs to be put on every couple of days and your dog will very quickly no longer chew your walls, doors, etc.

FREDAHOGAN

How to stop your dog chewing wood fittings in the house, when sprinkling black pepper doesn't work

Tabasco sauce – tiny bottle – very, very hot. Did this for our Staffordshire terrier when a puppy – stopped after first chew.

TOPTIPTWIN

How to stop your dog from licking the incision after an operation

My vet suggested putting a T-shirt on my dog. You put it on like you would on a person. She seemed happy with it and didn't lick the wound.

NICO

How to stop your dog jumping up at guests

Tell your guests to completely ignore the dog. Don't even look at it. It will then get less excited and shut up.

PGRIER

How to get your horse to trust you more

Here is an exercise to build trust between horse and owner. First, put the horse into a school and go in with him. Take off the halter and lead, and chase him off. Make him run circles around the pen until you see certain signs: his inside ear pointing towards the centre of the ring where you are standing and chewing movements with his mouth. Now stop chasing him and turn away. Wait until he walks to you. Make him follow you, then reward him.

SOCCERCHIC99

How to keep your pony's mane and tail clean and tangle-free

When the mane or tail is washed, brush in cheap furniture polish (we use Tesco Value) thoroughly. This not only keeps it tangle-free but also protects the mane/tail hair from dirt. I find it easier to spray the polish on to the brush and then brush the mane/tail. Repeat until all the hair is coated.

HDC1960

How to save time in the stables on a weekday

At the weekend, when you have more time, fill enough hay nets to last the week. I fill seven, one for each day, and if my horse is kept in due to bad weather, I fill the odd one during the week. Make up enough dry feeds for the week and put them into polythene bags. If you use Speedi-Beet, soak enough for the week – it will keep well in cold weather. I use four empty garlic tubs to mix the dry and wet feed, enough for two days. The stable girl gives one tub to my horse in the morning and one in the evening, along with a hay net. I muck out at the weekend, and on a Tuesday and Thursday. It takes me only about an hour to muck out and mix feeds during the week. I don't groom during the week, and just pick out his feet if required.

EDFIN

I have a small grooming kit in a trug-type bucket in the stable corner: just a couple of brushes and a hoof pick for quick flicks and a bottle of fly repellent for a quick spray, before turning out. At the back of the stable, I have tied and hung baling twine across two of the rafters, about three metres apart. I have slipped a strong drainpipe through the tied twine and I use this for hanging rugs on, to save the walk to the tack room. Keep everything as close to hand as possible.

COLIYTYHE

How to get rid of green algae in your rabbit's water bottles

Use sterilising fluid, such as Milton, and rinse out well.

BUMPY

How to keep rabbits cool

I put a bottle of frozen water in a football sock and they lie next to it when they need to be cooled down. Make sure their hutch/run has plenty of shade in it. If they drink from a bowl, you can put a couple of ice cubes in the water.

FEMME_FATALE

MONEY

or If banks were clever, they'd handwrite their envelopes –
then we'd actually open them

How to settle with collection agencies so your credit rating isn't affected

Don't bury your head in the sand; get in contact with the agency. They have dealt with many situations and will have an option that you can live with. Think about ways you can save money in everyday life that will help you pay your debts faster. If you have a large amount of debt, then debt counselling might be an idea – try the Citizens Advice Bureau. There is also great advice and support on the moneysavingexpert.com site and forums. Do NOT go to those consolidation companies or take advice from a loan/IVA provider – their objective is to get you to take more credit and there are other things you should consider first. Be proud of yourself for taking the first step to a debt-free existence, and be patient while it gets sorted.

CATRINE

How to get out of debt

Remember to focus the bulk of your monthly payments on credit cards on which you are paying interest. If you've any interest-free cards, just pay the minimum and concentrate on clearing the cards that are actively adding to your debt.

LINDACEE

How to get a loan when banks don't seem to be lending these days

Proof of being a low-risk credit customer with a good payment record on any car loans or credit card payments and a secure, salaried job will help. As would a financially sound guarantor who can guarantee your loan repayment.

CONNYOSB

How to save a lot of money at the supermarket

I discovered this top tip yesterday by accident! I popped out to the supermarket to do my weekly shop carrying only my debit card. Thinking I could grab a huge trolley and have a good browse, I found that all the trolleys needed a one pound coin. With no cash on me, I was forced to use a basket. Not only did I get round the shop quickly as my arms ached, but I also ended up spending a lot less than I would have had I been browsing. I also came home with exactly what was on the list!

RAEFAYE

How to save money when shopping

If you're shopping for food, eat before you shop. It's very simple and it works.

MADZ

How to save money on grocery shopping

If you always do your grocery shopping on the same day every week, try shopping one day later each week (with the same list), and over seven weeks you'll have saved one week's worth of your shopping.

AMONTANINI

My first stop in the supermarket is the section with the reduced items that are short-dated. Try to figure out what time they make their reductions – it may be 6.30 or 8 p.m., but it can be worth checking out and changing the way you shop.

ALLY1310

How to avoid impulse buying

I make a pre-shopping trip every season. I walk around the stores just to look at the new styles and what I will need. I don't carry more then twenty pounds in cash and I leave my credit card at home so I won't be tempted to overspend. I have no problem telling the sales girl that I'm just looking. This is when I'll try things on to see what brands fit well. Then I go back the next week with my credit card. It's amazing how many things are not as appealing when you wait a week.

MASI

How to save money when you're a teenager

If you go out for the day, take your own food. Goodness knows how much money I have wasted on things I can get from home for free! If I get money from relatives I put fifty per cent of it into my savings account.

S123

Maybe ask your mum to keep back part of your allowance and save it for you. It may hurt, but it's amazing how fast savings can mount up when you haven't seen the money in the first place.

LINDACEE

How to beat shopping addiction

Put your credit cards in a tin can filled with water and put it in the freezer. That way you can't put it in the microwave to thaw out. When you see that 'must-have' outfit, bag or pair of shoes, salivate over them, but don't buy yet. Tell yourself you will buy them in one week's time. During that week, think about the must-have item, imagine it in your wardrobe and how it will make your life complete. If after a week you still desire it as much as you did on day one, then buy it, but buy it out of your current account. If, however, you no longer feel so strongly about it, put that same amount of money in a savings account and see how good you feel about yourself.

ANNWAE

Avoid the shops. Sounds so simple, but it's so effective. If you have a lunch hour, take up reading a book in the canteen, or use it for a fitness jog or something similar. I used to go round the shops at lunch and it just put temptation in my way.

SCOTTISHCHIC

How to stop yourself from frittering away all your money on nothing

For one month, starting on payday, keep a diary of everything you buy, from the weekly shop to a thirty-five-pence chocolate bar! At the end of the month, look back and you will feel guilty/shocked about how much money you've pretty much thrown away. For the next month, move the amount you would normally spend on useless stuff from your current account to a savings account – your savings will build up in no time and you won't be tempted to spend. I've done this – it's hard to get used to but it's made such a huge difference to my and my partner's lifestyle.

SCOTTISHCHIC

How to save money on dry cleaning

Read the label in your clothes! If it says 'dry clean', it is just a suggestion and it means that you can wash the garment yourself – but do it carefully. If it says 'dry clean only', it is pretty much an order and you risk damaging the garment if you launder it any other way.

TOOKE

How to spend less on disposable swim nappies for babies and toddlers

Don't throw away your 'disposable' swim nappies. They will rinse through and dry so can be worn a few times. They can even be put through the washing machine on a gentle wash. Great for holidays as you don't need to take as many as you would if you were to chuck them out after each swim.

SPENDSPENDSPEND

How to save money on phone calls

Before you phone an expensive 0870 phone number go to SAYNOTO0870.COM and check out whether there is an alternative number.

ALLY1310

How to save money for your child when you are useless at saving and spend like there's no tomorrow

Open a child account in his or her own name so only he or she can access the money, and set up a direct debit from your account into it.

SQUIRREL

How to save money

Getting together with a few friends in similar financial circumstances and agreeing to save X amount of money every week is another way of saving. Like a diet club, if you can encourage and remind each other, you can do it. You could have that dress or holiday in no time.

LUCYD

If you're creating a budget for yourself, don't be too strict. It's a little bit like a rigid diet – if it's too extreme it only makes you more inclined to fall off the wagon! The more realistic you can be with your goals the better it will work.

LUCYD

HAPPINESS

or Don't postpone it

How to be happy

'It takes as much energy to wish as it does to plan,' said
Eleanor Roosevelt. Start making plans for something
you've only dreamt about so far.

ABI1973

Pay for the person behind you in the queue: at the
newsagent's, at the cafe, at the supermarket – whatever
you can easily afford.

TROOPS

Before bed, consider what you've done to be proud
of today and what you will do that you're proud of
tomorrow.

GRETCHEN

Bake something and take it to the office to share with
colleagues. There's nothing like home-made yummies to
spread happiness at work.

ESME

Smile. At everyone, everywhere. ALL DAY. Particularly
at strangers. Even if they look at you strangely.

LIBBYUK2003

Think of a compliment you would like to receive and act in a way that deserves it.

EMERALD

Expect the worst. You then get an uplift from the gap between the worst that you expected and the way that reality has turned out to be. Exaggerate the awfulness. It's a very British thing to do.

ALAIN DE BOTTON

I follow Mma Ramotswe's advice on the subject of happiness. She is quite clear on this; she says that the surest way to be happy is to cause happiness in others and then to enjoy it oneself. I think she is right.

ALEXANDER McCALL SMITH

I sometimes need to remind myself that my happiest times are when things are pretty simple, like a take-out on the kitchen table with family and friends (and a good bottle of wine). The message is, I think, don't over-complicate, as, often, you remember the mood not the detail. Oh, and being somewhere with good BlackBerry coverage!

ANYA HINDMARCH

Do not expect to be happy, then it might sneak up on you.

BEL MOONEY

Enjoy every minute.

BRENT HOBERMAN

My tip for happiness is to 'believe the best in everyone'. It's amazing, if you live by this mantra, how rarely you are disappointed, and it makes the world seem a much happier place.

CHARLES DUNSTONE

Cuddle more. Tickle more. Sleep more.

CLAUDIA WINKLEMAN

Swim at dawn on an empty Cornish beach.

DAVID CAMERON

Wear a fabulous smile, great jewellery and know that you are totally and utterly in control!

DONATELLA VERSACE

There's a Chinese proverb: 'Those the gods hate, they satisfy their ambitions.' I find that comforting because it implies that, ultimately, happiness is in the striving, not the succeeding.

JEMIMA KHAN

Nature is the one thing that sustains me. I think people don't put their feet enough on the earth. As Wordsworth said, 'Nature never did betray the heart that loved her.' And there's that wonderful saying by Sacheverell Sitwell: 'The birds sing on the trees for rich and poor.' That, and giggling with [my husband] Leo in bed in the morning, and a large drink in the evening.

JILLY COOPER

Things that make me happy: a glass of Jack Daniel's at the end of a crazy week, landing a pontoon start and wakeboarding behind a speedboat, a good massage from someone with firm hands and sitting on a beach as the sun goes down, watching my kids play in the sea. Wish I was enjoying one of those right now!

JO WHILEY

Work as if the money doesn't matter. Love as if you have never been broken-hearted. And dance as if no one else is watching.
PS Also, don't feel bad about pinching other people's ideas: I was given this advice by my dancing partner, Kristina Rihanoff.

JOHN SERGEANT

Read your kids a bedtime story.

VISCOUNT ROTHERMERE

In the words of Cole Porter, 'Make someone happy.' Happiness is also Twitter, family (sometimes!), sleep and a tidy house.

KIRSTIE ALLSOPP

Create something.

LUKE JOHNSON

Love and be loved.

MARTHA LANE FOX

Eat peanut butter and jam on toast.

NICK CLEGG

Eat, drink and nap.

NICK JONES

Don't take yourself too seriously.

NIKLAS ZENNSTRÕM

As Joseph Campbell said, 'Follow your bliss.'

PETER GABRIEL

Being with my sons.
Finishing a book.
Starting a book.
Being in the middle of a book.
Jameson on the rocks.
Vivian Blaine singing 'A Person Could Develop A Cold'
from the movie *Guys and Dolls*.
The Uffizi Museum.
The song 'Bombay Meri Jaan'.
The company of friends.
Watching Roger Federer play tennis.
Kindness.
New York City.
Bombay.

SALMAN RUSHDIE

Happiness is having a husband who makes you laugh.

SUE LAWLEY

Give your time to the people who matter most to you
and remember who you are irreplaceable to.

TESSA JOWELL

How to be happy is for me very easy! The biggest
pleasure anyone can give is by cooking a delicious home-
cooked meal; it always brings a smile to anyone's face.

TOM AIKENS

Think of yourself in the future, lying on your deathbed. You look back on your life and think:
(1) have I made the most of my life on this earth?
(2) did I do everything I could to make sure I was happy – big things and little things?
(3) did I make other people happy?
Then snap back into the present and be so very grateful you are not on your deathbed yet, and realise that we really do get only ONE life, which is very precious, so don't waste it being unhappy. Make every day count and start by deciding now, at this very minute, that you are going to be HAPPY, goddamit, regardless of what life throws at you. In the end, we will all end up the same way – life is for living, so start living it NOW!

WILLKAT

A life coach gave me this tip. When I wake up, I think to myself that today will be a great day and I am going to stay happy all day and just have fun. I didn't really believe her at the time until I tried it and it really does work.

LAURENFITZ

Try avoiding people who are often miserable and depressed. Keep with the smilers and enthusiasts. That doesn't mean you should ditch your best friend when her man chucks her and she genuinely needs a shoulder to cry on; it just means trying to stay away from the moaners until your spirits lift.

MINERVABYTES

(1) Be impeccable with your word, meaning tell the truth and don't gossip.
(2) Don't take anything personally. Everything anyone says, even if they say it about you, is about them, not about you.
(3) Don't make assumptions.
(4) Always do your best.

ASILDEM

Make a list of things you never complain about. It focuses your mind on all the things you are grateful for. They say, 'Change your attitude and you change the world.' It works!

BRIDGET

Make a real effort in planning and doing those things that will make you feel happier and better about yourself, such as a charitable act, doing something nice for a friend, a fun outing, challenging yourself with a new hobby, etc. So many people make plans for the other aspects of their lives but think that happy moments occur only by happenstance or accident. There's no reason why you can't do something concrete and actually form plans to make your life generally happier.

JILLAROO95

This quote really resonated with me: 'There comes a time in life when you have to let go of all the pointless drama and the people who create it, and surround yourself with people who make you laugh so hard that you forget the bad, and focus solely on the good. After all, life is too short to be anything but happy.' Remember, no matter how much it may feel that it's not the case, YOU (and no one else) are responsible for your own happiness. If you are not happy, work out what the problem is, and solve it.

LEILU

LIFE

or Any other business

Great ideas for April Fools' Day

Turn every battery from every appliance in the house
the wrong way round, including the TV remote, mouse,
radios, power tools, anything.

ABII1973

The night before, put all the clocks in your house
forward an hour and lie back and listen as everyone else
panics in the morning.

ESME

The night before, add food colouring to the milk in your
fridge.

JOANG

How to be good

If it's not nice, not true and not necessary, don't say it.

GEMINI

How to deal with a group of young boys playing football in the street right outside your house

Try dropping stink bombs (which you can buy from any
good joke shop) in the area. Although you might have to
put up with the smell for a bit, it will see them off.

S123

How to get neighbours to quieten down

I have had neighbours who regularly held noisy parties in their garden late at night. I would then open my windows and play either classical or cheesy music quite loudly – they soon got the message.

ENGLISHCHICK

How to develop better handwriting

My mum always said that the key to neat handwriting was to keep all the letters the same size, so that the tops of the 'a', 'e', 'o', 'u', 'y', 'n', etc., are all in a straight line. Sounds simple but it's true.

ALIFLUMP

How to get revenge on a bitchy person when ignoring her doesn't work

A simple 'My, aren't we being rude/grumpy/bitchy today' has worked for me in the past, or 'I see you are flexing your inner bitch/witch today, well done.' Don't shout it, but say it loud enough so you can be heard – hopefully by a few people, including your bitchy person.

VALENTINE

How to get rid of pushy salesmen

If he's one of those dreaded people on the doorstep wanting you to change your energy supplier (or something equally irritating), just wait for a pause in the spiel and politely say, 'I'm not interested, thank you, and I'm shutting the door now.' If he's actually in your house, one of the best weapons you can use is silence.

LINDACEE

How to give a sincere apology

Eye contact – no matter how hard it is, look the person in the eye.

MEGALLE925

Think about exactly what you did wrong and why it was wrong. Say these points first. Explain that you know you were wrong. Follow up a verbal apology with a written one. Under no circumstances make a joke. After the apology allow the other person some time to think before you contact him or her again. Do not ask if you're forgiven.

CHARLIAMIO

How to respond to a rude question

I ask for the question to be repeated. Mentally, you can smack the person with an invisible spade, but in reality, it is best to say, 'Could you repeat the question?' You can then reply, 'Why do you want to know?' This is polite, yet it will probably make the person blush as he or she will look rude and crass to the people around you.

BAKEWELL

How to prevent glasses from steaming up when boarding a bus in cold weather

If you can see without them for a bit, put them in your pocket before or after getting on the bus, so that they get used to the heat more quickly.

xXxLEANNExXx

How to cope with turning thirty-six

Think of the alternative to not turning thirty-six. We all know people who have died young; what's not to celebrate? If you are feeling bad about hitting thirty-six (you young thing), then take the opportunity to rethink your life, career, relationship/s, etc. If there's anything you don't like about your life, try to make small changes to improve it.

COLIYTYHE

How to feel more attractive again when you're in your forties and feel so old that responsibilities get the better of you and make you feel unsexy and boring

Why don't you do something 'naughty', like taking pole-dancing lessons? Enlist a couple of girlfriends and go and have a great giggle, while toning up your backside – both are guaranteed to make you feel more alive and sexy. And the great thing about being in your forties is that you can FINALLY do something fun like this without being crippled by teenage self-consciousness, or worrying for a second what the rest of the world thinks!

BooBoo

How to feel attractive when you're happily single, scrub up well, but are in your mid-forties

This is tough, but it helps to focus the mind: you will never be younger than you are today, your hair will only get greyer, your skin will only get more wrinkly. So, if you think about it, you're peaking! Make the most of it and don't waste a day.

VIVIAN

How to celebrate turning forty – without breaking the bank!

You might want to make the celebration occur over a year: make a list of things you've always wanted to do but have never got around to doing (for example, reading a particular classic you've never got through before, learning how to knit, running five miles non-stop, making a perfect soufflé, building a piece of furniture, etc.). Then work on one of these each month of your birthday year and make it a year of achievement.

JILLAROO95

How to teach yourself to act responsibly and think before acting

Start by deliberately waiting at least one full breath each and every time you have to answer a question/make a move/make a choice. That one breath may seem like a long time to pause and consider what you're doing, but it saves lots of time later in regret.

TIPTOETIPSTER

How to appear calm when you're burning up with rage

In an ideal world, relax your body. If you're too angry to do that, then try to stop obvious parts of your body from clenching up (e.g. fists or jaw) and transfer that tension to somewhere the other person can't see (e.g. curl up toes or clench buttocks). Biting the inside of your lip can force you to stop clenching your jaw, which is a real give-away. Make your eyes smile slightly – not too much or you look like a maniac, just enough so you appear relaxed and confident. Unless you're feeling calm enough, don't smile with your mouth, it will freeze and make you look more anxious/angry. Concentrate on relaxing your belly so that the breath can go all the way into your lungs, which will help calm you down anyway.

FEEBZI52

How to deal with short-fused people

Walk away after saying that you aren't going to talk to them while they are shouting/swearing, etc. Usually there is no reasoning with such people. You have to walk away and give them time to think better about what they are doing.

DOZIGGY

How to be less argumentative

This may sound lame but it really works. Whenever you feel angry or as though you're about to start an argument, do a slow count from ten backwards in your head, then take a deep breath and just talk calmly or walk away.

NICKIEBABESX

How to stop complaining and start enjoying life

I think, to a great degree, we're all in a position to decide whether or not we're going to be happy people. Try not to dwell on the stuff that's wrong in your life. The phrase 'count your blessings' is a bit hackneyed, but it's true. Concentrate on all the things that are good in your life, like great family/good friends/nice house/good job, etc. You do yourself no favours by being negative and pessimistic, and it's a sure-fire way to drive people away from you.

LindaCee

How to cope with bereavement

How close you were to the deceased will dictate pretty much how you cope. The closer you were, the harder it is. It is over three years since my young son died and I don't feel anywhere near coping with it really. Allow yourself time, and accept there is no right or wrong way to act or react. Don't be afraid to tell friends if you're having a bad day/time, and let them help. You will be told that everything you feel is normal and you'll feel like hitting that person, but it is true, there are so many emotions you have to go through, and so many different stages.

BUT one piece of advice – live! Make sure you make the most of your life in honour of your lost loved one. Live for them.

COLIYTYHE

Be honest, but brief, when people ask you how you are. If you always put a brave face on, people won't be so eager to offer help. Equally, if you give them an hour's commentary on why you are so miserable, they won't come back. Don't be afraid to ask for practical help, especially in the early days, and be specific. For instance, ask people to take you out and amuse you for the day, so you are forced to interact with the world again and remind yourself that life goes on, even if you are not yet ready to move on with it.

VILLANOVA

How to write a condolence/sympathy note

If you knew the deceased, you should always write to their loved ones. Notes and letters offer comfort many months later.

COOKIE

My father passed away in 1994, and the words from one note I received still stay with me to this day: 'I know how difficult this is to accept.' The note was from someone who had just lost her own father, and I can't tell you how much it touched me. It is indeed so hard to believe that the person you've loved your whole life is really gone. I've used those seven words in many sympathy notes since then. I hope they help you too.

SUSIEQ76

How to make yourself more comfortable making eye contact with people

Look at the space between their eyes instead of trying to look into both eyes. I have the same problem and no one EVER notices!

JESSYIDOL

How to be more assertive. I can't say no when asked for favours, then feel resentful towards my friends or family

This just takes practice and the trick is to say no. Just no or 'sorry, I can't'. No further explanation as to why you can't. You may have to repeat the 'sorry, I just can't' sentence a few times before people get the idea. It worked for me. If you're not happy saying this, then say, 'I will have to think about it and will get back to you shortly.' It's the long-winded explanations of why you can't do something that make you feel trapped into saying yes.

ASHLING

How to become confident

Don't know if this will 'give' you confidence, but I was on the beach when I heard a little girl ask her mum to take her to the toilet. Mum said, 'You can go on your own.' She said, 'But everyone will look at me', and Mum replied, 'If they do, it's because you are beautiful!' I had to smile.

ALI161

How to boost your self-esteem

I think you need to look outside yourself. Find ways to contribute to others, through charities, church, your children's school, etc. By helping others or contributing to projects, you will forget about whether you are adequate or not, and have concrete evidence (when you find time to look) of your value. You will also be setting a good example for your children and they will enjoy a more well-rounded parent.

HJASON

How to draw attention to yourself

Greet people, even if you don't know them, and they will notice you for the rest of the evening.

DINE

How to get people to notice you and like you more

Relax. Stop being so self-conscious. And read some interesting books so you have intriguing things to say.

JOSA2

How to make a good first impression

When entering a room, push the door handle down before you begin opening it, rather than pushing down and forward all at once. This should ensure you come into the room with your face tilted upwards and your body rising, rather than falling downwards.

FEEBZI52

How to overcome shyness

The thing with shyness is that it tends to go away once you've actually taken your first step. Try easing yourself into whatever you're shy of. For example, if you're shy of approaching people, make it your business to say something to five strangers a day, even if it's just 'Good morning!' or 'Wow, isn't the view brilliant!' Close your eyes, take a deep breath, and say to yourself, 'Nothing bad will happen to me', then go do it. What's the worst that could happen?

ESTUANS_INTERIUS

How to begin a conversation with the very old or ill

Try, 'Can I ask your advice about something?' Just invent a problem – how to roast a chicken, where is the best place to shop, does my bum look big in this, anything you like. Being asked for advice is a friendly compliment to someone. It makes them feel useful and knowledgeable. The old are frequently on the receiving end of the helping hand through no fault of their own and it would give people a lift to know that they are valued and still able to help the world go round.

LADYDIGGER

My father is ninety-seven and his only grumble is that he feels so helpless and useless when he sees someone (usually me) doing something he feels unable to do, like the gardening. Asking his advice on lots of levels (whether or not I need it) makes him feel valued and wise (which he is). Remember how much more old people know than we do.

DOINGMYBEST

How to find interesting subjects to talk about

My no-fail conversation-starter is natural disasters. When I'm with people I don't know very well, I bring this up. It gets interesting, particularly when you talk to people from different areas. I live in earthquake country and have had all sorts of interesting conversations with folks comparing the experience of living with earthquakes versus living with other disasters. Once, I was at a conference and sitting at a large, round table with a bunch of people I didn't know. I started the conversation and, eventually, our table was three-people thick with others who wanted to join in. And I've had similar results whenever I've used this as a conversation-starter.

JILLAROO95

How to stop yourself crying in public

Pushing your tongue to the roof of your mouth hard works well, and try rubbing hard above your upper lip – this also works for some reason.

HEFZI

If you're arguing a point, just remember that you lose a massive amount of ground as soon as you start to cry. Keep control and you'll be taken a whole lot more seriously.

LINDACEE

How to know how much to gamble

If you cannot afford to give it away, then don't gamble it.

CATRINE

Don't gamble, buy shoes!

FLUFFYFOX

How to cope with loneliness

I remember only too well a time in my life when I felt so lonely and it was awful. I took on a second job in a bar to make extra cash and get out of the grotty flat I lived alone in. I also applied to be an adult helper on the adult literacy scheme run by most local councils. I felt I was helping other people, which gave me a sense of satisfaction, and I was earning a few extra pounds in the bar and had somewhere else to go rather than staying in my flat alone.

NUMPTIEHEID

How to be better at waking up and getting out of bed in the morning

If you can open your eyes or be somewhat conscious, then get up ASAP. I find that if I walk around and even leave my room, the need to get back into bed will fade. If you can get to the kitchen without hurting yourself in your half-awake state, even better.

2SQRRD

How to have enough time to complete day-to-day tasks when it seems you never get anything done

Set yourself one task at a time, and give yourself time to do it, say twenty minutes. Set a timer clock for this time and crack on. You will be surprised how much you get through.

REDLADY

How to deal with a prank phone call

Buy a whistle and blow it as hard as you can down the phone. They will get the message.

BEKKI007

Look up the procedure for reporting such calls to your local police and phone company. During the next call, say something like, 'I have contacted my local police and telephone company to report these harassing phone calls. Cease and desist or I shall take all available legal action against you.' Then hang up, and do not engage in dialogue. If you feel it is appropriate (these calls can be scary and make you feel stalked), DO contact the police and phone company. They can trace numbers (even ones your caller ID cannot) and take action. Once you've complained, calls can best be traced at the time they are made, so don't wait if the calls are getting frightening.

DezG

Just lay the receiver down and leave it. As the person receiving the call, it's up to you to cut it off, so keep the caller waiting as long as possible – hopefully running up their bill. You could even say, 'Your call is important to us, sorry to keep you waiting.'

Ally1310

How to look good in photos

Point your chin slightly down and angle your face to the side a little. Look at the person taking the picture (a few inches above the camera) and your eyes will look a little bigger, without red eye.

BAKEWELL

Look into the camera and say, 'Hi, there!' really enthusiastically, as though you've just seen a great friend. It really works.

TOOKE

How to be confident singing in front of people

My mother, who was an opera singer, always told
me to put my hand on the corner of the piano, or to
hold something small that fitted in the palm of my
hand. I don't know why this worked, but it did. It
took my mind off the people in front of me. Instead, I
concentrated on rolling this thing in my hand.

PIENKFLY

How to learn to float

First, you have to be comfortable in the water – having
water in your ears, letting it splash on your face, etc.
Stand in shallow water so you don't panic. Next, have a
friend support you as you recline back on to the water
(his hands on your lower back/bum and shoulders). Lie
in the water with your feet outstretched and your arms
forming a 'T' shape or above your head, stick your belly
out, and don't let your bum drop. Lie there supported
by your friend until you are comfortable. Then tell your
friend to let go slowly (moving his hands away and
causing you to feel less hand pressure, more float). You're
floating! (May take several tries.)

DEZG

A simple tip from me: bum up and ears in the water – it
keeps your body level.

LINDACEE

How to overcome apprehension

If you're terrified or even phobic about a future event, such as the dentist or a visit to the shops, try this: repeat in your mind or even out loud what you are afraid of, such as 'I've got to go the dentist', for about fifteen minutes, and before you know it, your mind has wandered on to something else. It takes the terror out of the thought.

BRADLEY

When you start to feel anxious, do some deep breathing, the out breaths should be longer than the in breath. Ideally, a count of seven on the in breath and eleven on the out breath.

AKB

How to stop worrying about everything and just enjoy life

A good way to put things into perspective is to ask yourself: 'How much will this matter six months from now?'

MAGDA

INDEX